ATLANTIC

OCEAN

EUROPE

AFRICA

INDIAN

OCEAN

SOUTH

AMERICA

Barbados

SURINAM

Panama Canal

Ascension

MADAGASCAR
(MALAGASY)

Cocos Is.

Port
Louis

Mauritius
La Réunion

Cape Town

Durban
East London
Port Elizabeth

Cape of Good Hope

S0-ARC-427

W. K. Plummer

The Boy
Who Sailed Around
the World Alone

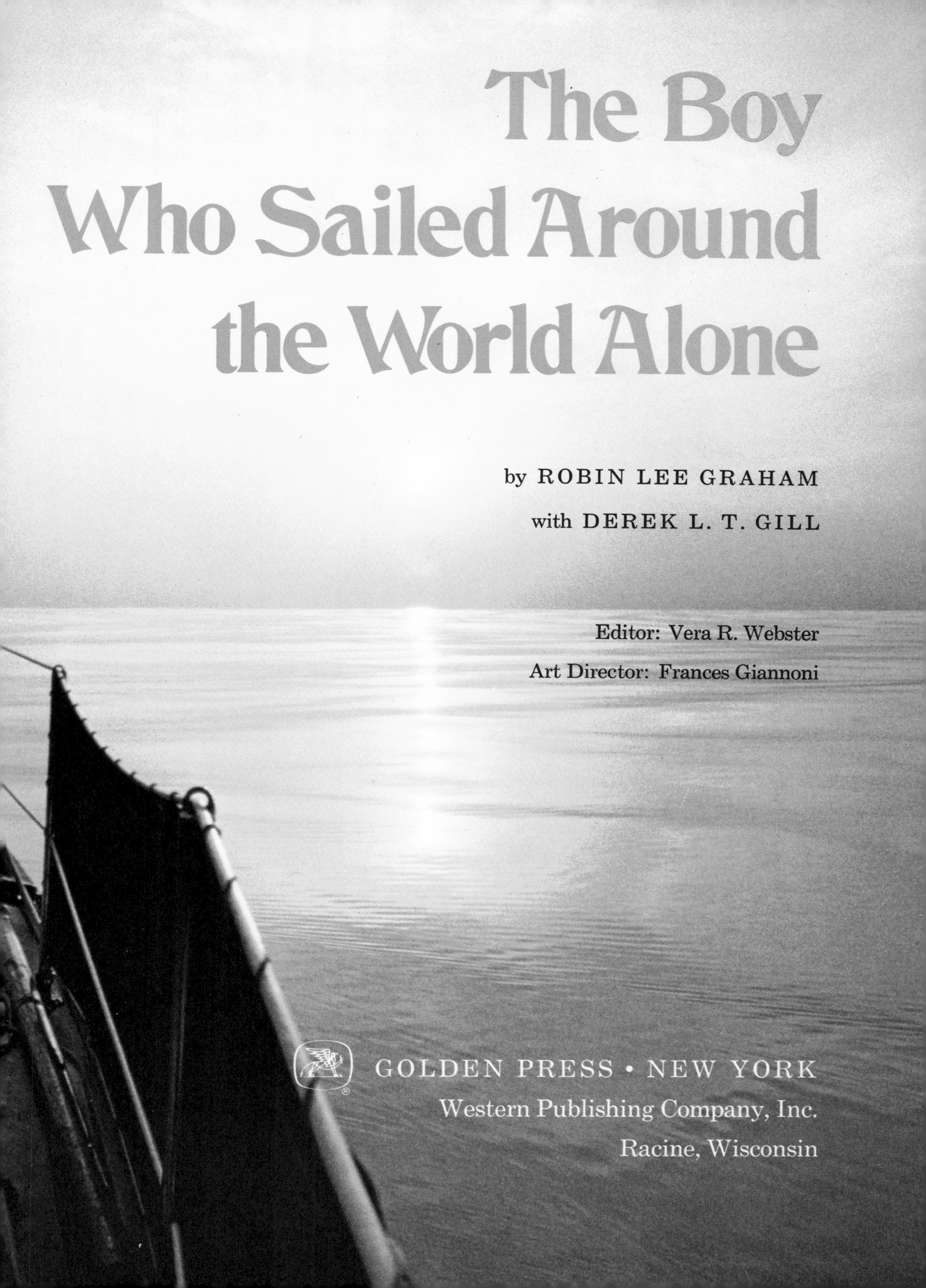

The Boy
Who Sailed Around
the World Alone

by ROBIN LEE GRAHAM

with DEREK L. T. GILL

Editor: Vera R. Webster

Art Director: Frances Giannoni

GOLDEN PRESS • NEW YORK
Western Publishing Company, Inc.
Racine, Wisconsin

Acknowledgments

In the preparation of any book, the cooperation and efforts of many people are involved. It is for that reason that I should like to take this opportunity to thank those who would not otherwise be acknowledged. I should like to thank Mr. Herbert S. Wilburn, Illustrations Director for the *National Geographic Magazine*, who helped secure for us the permission to reprint photographs that had previously appeared in the *National Geographic Magazine*. I should also like to thank Robin's parents, Mr. and Mrs. Lyle Graham, for giving us access to their family albums and other personal records, and for supplying us with many of the photographs that appear in this book.

In addition to the many photographs that were supplied by Robin Lee Graham and his father, Mr. Lyle Graham, the following list of photographers are to be credited also: Walter Aguiar, pp. 14 and 123 (*top right and top left*); Ted Bachelor, p. 70 (*top left*); Cloud Chart, Inc., pp. 16-17; Harold Edgerton, p. 42; James R. Holland, pp. 116, 117, 118 (*top and bottom*); Robert W. Madden, pp. 139 (*top and bottom*) and 138 (*right*); and Donald G. Schultz, p. 112. Pictures copyrighted by the National Geographic Society are credited wherever they appear. And especially, I should like to thank Linda Neilson for the careful selection and painstaking effort she put into the mechanical structuring of each page layout in coordinating text with pictures.

Vera R. Webster
EDITOR

*This book is dedicated
to my Dad who taught me a love
of the sea and adventure,
to my Mom who allowed me to go,
and to Patti who gave me courage
to finish the voyage.*

Table of Contents

My tenth birthday present was a real sailing boat, a dinghy with a mast. I sailed a boat for the first time.

Scuba diving too was a part of my early training for adventures at sea.

CHAPTER I

My First Boat

ON THE WALL of my bedroom there was a picture of a sailboat. When I closed my eyes, I pretended to climb aboard. I could almost hear the waves lapping against the hull and the sound of the wind in the rigging.

Of course, when I opened my eyes again, the picture boat had not moved at all, but it seemed to be waiting just for me.

Soon it would be my tenth birthday. I had a quick answer when my Mom and Dad asked me what I would like most.

"A boat!" I said. "A real sailboat!"

Mom looked surprised. "Don't be silly," she said. "Can't you think of anything you'd really like?"

Dad just laughed.

We were living near the sea at Morro Bay. This is a little town on the Pacific coast, about halfway between San Francisco and Los Angeles. My birthday was on March 5. At breakfast time that day, before I went to school, I unwrapped some presents that had been put around my place at the table. Mostly they were pretty dull—a pen and pencil set, a new sweater and a baseball bat. My brother Michael, who is five years older than I am, gave me the bat. He was good at baseball. I guess he wanted to get me interested in playing too.

What puzzled me was that there was no present from Mom and Dad. All Dad said was, "Remember, Robin, it will still be your birthday this afternoon."

When I got back from school, my parents were waiting for me. They asked me to go with them to the end of the garden, where there was an old wooden jetty half covered in reeds. Tied up to the jetty was a little dinghy with a mast. The boat was like the one in the picture in my bedroom, except that it had a red sail.

Mom and Dad were looking at me and smiling happily.

So on my tenth birthday I sailed a boat for the first time, but I didn't sail alone. Dad got into the dinghy with me, and he had brought along a book called *How to Sail Small Boats*. When we had raised the sail, the dinghy was like a puppy sighting a squirrel. As soon as we had untied the dinghy, we were out in the bay. Dad was reading the handbook aloud on how to handle a small boat and he had just got to the paragraph about jibing. We did not know what jibing meant, but we soon discovered. We were starting to go downwind (sailing with the wind) and had the sail way out. Suddenly, the boom was thrown across the boat and we

I longed to be as free as the seagulls, and from them I learned how to judge the strength and direction of the wind.

capsized and had to swim ashore. So I had had my first important lesson in sailing. I had learned that sailing could be dangerous as well as fun.

Soon I was out sailing by myself. After school each day, when other kids went off to play Little League baseball, I would run down to the wooden jetty and take out the dinghy.

With the seagulls diving and squawking about me, I began to understand that one of the first secrets to controlling a sailboat is to know the direction and the strength of the wind.

Sudden changes in the wind can make sailing quite difficult—and exciting. To help me find the direction of the wind, I tied a red ribbon to the top of the dinghy's mast. Sailors call these wind indicators "telltales." I learned how important it was to keep an eye on my telltale. I watched the seagulls, too—how, when they flew against the wind, they

hovered like helicopters, and when flying with the wind, they flashed past.

A sailboat can never sail directly into the wind. About the closest it can go is 45 degrees. If you put your watch flat on a table and you think of the wind coming towards you from twelve o'clock, then the closest a sailboat can move into the wind is ten o'clock or two o'clock. To sail in the direction of the wind you have to sail (tack) to port (left) and starboard (right).

I began to pick up words that sailors use. For example, if the wind is coming directly from the side—that is, from three o'clock or nine o'clock on your watch—it is said to be coming "off the beam."

A boat will lean over most when it is traveling to windward. The most relaxing and pleasant sailing is when the wind is on the beam. Then you don't get wet from spray, as you always do when going to windward, and you don't have to worry about jibing. A boat travels at its best speed when the wind is on the stern quarter—say at four o'clock or eight o'clock on your watch.

When the wind is directly behind you (aft), the sailor talks of scudding or running with the wind. On bigger yachts this is the time when you put out the balloon-like spinnaker.

But running with the wind is also the most dangerous sailing because this is when a boat can jibe. A small boat can tip over, a big boat can lose its mainmast, and if the boom swings across unexpectedly, it can give you a bad crack on the head.

My little dinghy had only one sail, so it was easy to handle and to change direction. Managing a dinghy is the best way to learn about sailing. Of course, sailboats with two and three sails go much faster. I wasn't worried about speed because I had more time to learn about basic seamanship.

I learned how much clouds can tell you about the weather. Even the color of the sky can give warning of the kind of weather to expect. The sailor's rhyme goes:

A red sky in the morning
Is the sailor's warning.
A red sky at night
Is the sailor's delight.

Another rhyme the sailor knows goes:

Evening red and morning gray
Are sure signs of a fine day.

This ancient warning comes from the Book of St. Matthew in the Bible.

As I walked to school each morning, or before going to bed at night, I began to "read" the sky.

Most often a red sky in the morning means that wind and rain are on the way. A yellow sunset usually means wind is coming. A misty gray morning indicates that the

The sky has many faces. From it I learned the kind of weather to expect, whether fair or foul, calm or stormy.

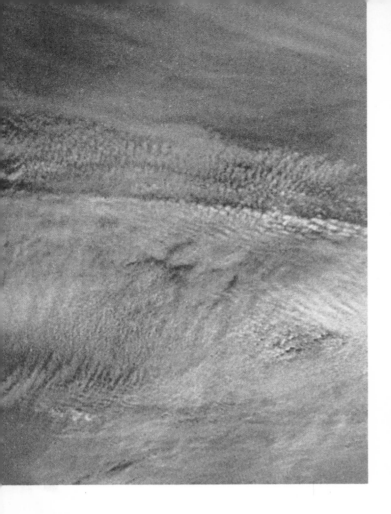

Cirrocumulus—a change in the weather.

Cirrus clouds—if they move, head for home.

weather is going to be calm and safe for sailing, but if the horizon looks a bit brown, it is a warning of fog. I found out later that the sky has different ways of giving signals in different parts of the world.

Most of the different kinds of clouds have long names. For instance, the white flaky clouds which have no shadows and which often stretch out in thin strips are called cirrocumulus. They usually mean there is going to be a change in the weather. The high feathery clouds which sometimes move together toward one point on the horizon are known as cirrus. If the cirrus start to move quickly, it is a warning to make for home. They can build up into a thunderstorm. But if the cirrus clouds are lazy and begin to vanish as the sun rises, the weather is likely to be fine and dandy.

The big white woolly clouds that look as if you could bounce on them are called cumu-lus. They indicate fair, perhaps breezy weather. But if the cumulus start to grow dark and are on the windward side, then they are a warning to make for home because there is likely to be a heavy rainstorm.

Nimbostratus are those thick dark clouds, low in the sky. They almost always mean wet weather and that wind is coming.

The danger warnings to the sailor are the cumulonimbus clouds. They often look like mountains. Aircraft pilots avoid them. They mean strong wind and thunder.

Tides played a big role in sailing in Morro Bay because at low tide there would be no water in the bay except in channels. Many times I would have to push the boat through waist-deep mud to get home. Tides can make a big difference to the speed of sailing if you are near to land. Before I began sailing, I was bored when someone tried to explain to me the cause of tides. But when I found how

16

Cumulus—clouds you want to bounce on.

Cumulonimbus—pilots keep clear of these.

useful tides can be or how annoying, I wanted to learn the reason for tides.

It fascinated me that tides are caused by the "pull" of the sun and the moon—mostly the moon. Twice each 24 hours the sea surges out of the bays and away from the beaches and then, after a short pause, it surges back again towards the coast. Because the moon rises about 50 minutes later every day, the times of the high tide and the low tide change by about 50 minutes each day. It is obviously much easier to sail out from the coast when the tide is going out, and easier to sail home when the tide is coming in.

Where the incoming tide meets the outgoing tide there is almost always rough water. The first time I took the dinghy into this meeting place of the tides the dinghy very nearly capsized.

Currents also affect sailing and they are found even in the deepest oceans and hundreds of miles from land. There are many reasons for currents, but coastal currents are usually caused by rivers or inlets pouring their water into the sea.

Every day I learned something new about the sea. And because I wanted to understand things like why the sea is salty and who were the first people to sail the oceans, my school work improved too. Because I wanted to read a compass and to discover how sailors find their positions when far from land, I took more interest in math.

I looked at my atlas and learned the names of places far away. I tried to picture myself in a sailboat making voyages to distant lands, perhaps even to Australia, Africa and South America.

Although I did not know it at the time, I was preparing myself for a great adventure. I was going to be the youngest sailor to sail around the world alone.

CHAPTER II

The *Golden Hind*

MY PARENTS had made me promise two things. The first was that I would always wear a life jacket in case I fell overboard or the boat capsized, and secondly, that I would never sail out into the open sea.

I often sailed to the mouth of Morro Bay where the swell suddenly increased, and I began to long to sail into the ocean.

I said to myself, "One day, Robin Lee Graham, you are going to sail over that horizon." It was a sort of vow, I guess.

On a Saturday afternoon, when my Dad was helping me give the dinghy a new coat of paint, I told him about my dream of sailing the ocean. Dad put down the paintbrush and looked at me hard. He said, "Robin, if you want to do anything badly enough you will do it." Then he told me that when he was a boy he too had had a dream that he would sail around the world. Dad and my uncle had started to build an ocean-sailing yacht in their yard. The yacht was nearly completed when the Japanese bombed Pearl Harbor. Dad joined the Air Force and the backyard boat was sold. Now Dad wiped the paint off his hands and said, "Perhaps, Robin, you will fulfill my dream."

My father was a realtor and a building contractor. One Sunday morning Dad and I drove down to Long Beach, and walked on the marina. I had never seen so many sailboats. The masts looked like a forest of trees.

As we passed a 36-foot ketch called the *Golden Hind,* I noticed a big "For Sale" sign nailed to her side. Nobody was about so I jumped aboard. The *Golden Hind* was named for Sir Francis Drake's famous boat. I peered inside the cabin, which was big enough for six people. I invited Dad to come and take a look.

Three days later we were having dinner when Dad put down his fork and said quietly, "I have sold my business and I have bought the *Golden Hind.*" He paused, then added, "For the next year we are all going to go sailing and exploring in the South Seas."

For a moment we were so silent that you could have heard a spider walk across the floor. It is funny how you can remember little things so clearly. I remember how Mom started to pour salt into her coffee.

"A year at sea! Wow! That means no school," I shouted.

"Oh, no it doesn't," said Dad. "You are going to be taking your schoolbooks with you, and you are going to have to work at them every day."

I was now thirteen. None of us had ever sailed further than Catalina Island, 20 miles

Mom, Dad, Michael and I take to the sea aboard the Golden Hind, *the boat on which we spent a year sailing and exploring the South Seas. It was a year of fun and adventure and a lot of learning.*

The Polynesians were happy people, always laughing. It was easy to make friends with them.

I learned to read a sextant for I was to be the navigator.

The Golden Hind anchored in Robinson Cove, Papetoai Bay, Moorea.

off the coast from Los Angeles. That night Michael and I got out the big atlas and began to look up names of islands and places in the South Pacific—romantic names like Rangiora, Papeete, Tuamotu, Bora Bora, Moorea, Raratonga, Pago Pago.

We sailed the *Golden Hind* back to Morro Bay, and during the next few weeks Mom bought provisions, including 600 cans of food—"just in case we get stuck on a desert island," she said. Dad studied charts of the prevailing winds and currents and he arranged for our passports and other documents. Michael, who was crazy about dune-buggies, worked on the yacht's gasoline engine. Dad learned about navigation from a book, and he showed me how to read a sextant. I was to be the navigator. "And you'd better be good, or we may find ourselves at the South Pole," Dad warned.

So many things have happened to me since our voyage on the *Golden Hind* that memory of the adventure begins to fade. But I do remember being stuck in the doldrums for 18 days. The doldrums are the windless belts which circle the world north and south of the equator. Sailors hate the doldrums. The sails usually hang down like shirts in a closet. Sometimes we would sail only 30 miles in a day—unless we used the engine. Sailboats don't carry much fuel. The engine is meant to be used for emergencies or when getting in and out of harbor.

I have some happy memories of the *Golden Hind* adventure. I could never forget the beautiful Polynesian lagoons and how the lovely island girls in their brilliant *pereus* (dresses) would come running down the golden beaches, their arms filled with flowers and fresh fruit. At one of the Tuamotu Islands we made friends with a native family who showed us where to dive for shells and where to fish.

The Polynesian people always seemed to be laughing. They just love life. When we went to say goodbye to the Polynesian family, the father asked my parents if they would swap me for two of their young daughters, Joliette and Suzette. They said they wanted a blond-haired son. I liked the idea of the swap and of surfing and fishing every day for the rest of my life. My parents solemnly thanked the Polynesian family for their generous offer but they turned it down. Mom explained, "We will have to keep Robin because he's going to be our navigator."

Our family voyage in the *Golden Hind* took 13 months. My parents made me work at my schoolbooks every day, but I learned much more about our world—at least one corner of it—than I could learn from schoolbooks. I learned, for instance, that people with very little money, people who live in little grass shacks, can be happier than many people who live in big houses with swimming pools and who drive big cars.

I really began to love nature—the beauty of shells, the fantastic different kinds of fish that live in clear, unpolluted water.

The *Golden Hind* voyage was not all fun. We were 120 miles from the nearest surgeon in Papeete when I got an awful tummy ache. We just made the Papeete hospital in time before my appendix burst. I had to spend several weeks in the hospital after the operation because the wound would not heal properly.

On the return trip to California, I took on more and more of the navigation. Fortunately my father was always checking my calculations, otherwise I might have sailed the *Golden Hind* onto some rocks. But thanks to my father's coaching, I was becoming quite useful with a sextant by the time we arrived home with great suntans and lots of stories for our relatives and friends.

CHAPTER III

Lost in a Storm

IT WAS really hard to go back to school again and to settle down. In the summer vacation my father sold the *Golden Hind* and bought another ketch, *Valerie*. She was six feet shorter than the *Golden Hind* and easier to handle. Mom had had enough sailing, and my brother Michael couldn't take off time because he was going to college. Dad invited me to be his mate and to sail with him to Hawaii, a voyage of 2,200 miles which we completed in 28 days. This voyage added much to my seamanship experience because we weathered several storms and we took watch turn and turn about. It felt pretty good to be in charge of *Valerie* while Dad was sleeping.

I have one vivid memory of this voyage. A genoa sail packed in a canvas bag which was lying on the deck slid overboard. We turned *Valerie* about to scoop up the sail, but just as we came alongside it the canvas bag began to sink. Under a few inches of clear water, and perhaps because of the angle of the sun, the sinking bag looked like a human body with a white face. I was really scared, but I think the accident was another important lesson for me, for I gained a new respect for the sea. The ocean had always seemed to be my playground, sparkling and beautiful. But now I knew that the ocean could destroy without mercy. The ocean is a good example of "the beauty and the beast."

Dad had decided to start up a new business in Hawaii, so he sent me off to McKinley High School in Honolulu. My mother was still in California packing up our home on the mainland.

This Hawaiian school was my sixth school and so I had to make new friends all over again. Two brothers at McKinley became my close friends because they loved sailing almost as much as I did. Art was fourteen and Jim was fifteen, as I now was. We pooled our savings and bought a beat-up old 16-foot aluminum lifeboat for $100.

At every school lunch break, Jim, Art and I met in the shade of a palm tree where we talked about our boat which we called *HIC*. Secretly we began to plan to sail *HIC* to the South Sea Islands. We had been reading the stories of Huckleberry Finn as class assignments, but our own planned adventure seemed just as exciting as his.

HIC had not been used as a lifeboat for many years and she was full of holes. We had not gotten enough money to buy the special filling material at a marine shop but we discovered that chewing-gum was good for stopping leaks. To turn *HIC* into a sailing boat

Dad's new boat, Valerie, *is a cross between a cruiser and a racing boat. She has a nine foot beam and carries a main, jib, mizzen, Genoa and downwind sails. Dad and I sailed to Hawaii in 28 days.*

we made a mast from a boom we had salvaged from a wrecked yacht. We collected quite a lot of material, like wire rope, from the bottom of Ala Wai harbor. All we had to do was to dive for it.

Our biggest job was to make a keel. A sailboat has to have a keel or it can't be steered. We constructed our keel from plywood and bolted it to the hull. *HIC's* sails were just old throwaways from an abandoned ketch.

We went diving for more "treasure" from sunken boats at Ala Wai harbor—things like brass fittings which we could sell to the marine shop. When we had saved enough money we bought canned food to last us for two or three weeks. We figured that we would soon find a cove on Lanai Island where we could fish for our food and perhaps find fruit growing wild.

It was a Friday in January when Jim, Art and I tore pages from our school notebooks and wrote letters to our parents. We wanted our parents to receive the letters after we had set out on our adventure.

One of the oldest sailors' superstitions is never to start a voyage on a Friday. To do so means you will be unlucky. But it was on a Friday, just after school had finished, when we ran together down to the yacht harbor to start our adventure. We mailed our letters to our parents and then pushed *HIC* into the water. As we sailed past the breakwater we noticed that the small craft warning had been hoisted. This warning is a red pennant which warns of winds of up to 38 miles per hour. Most small craft—and *HIC* was very small—head for port when this warning goes up. We debated what we should do, turn back or continue on our way.

"If we do turn back now," I said, "how are we going to explain those letters to our parents?"

HIC, *the patched up lifeboat in which my friends and I ran away to sea.*

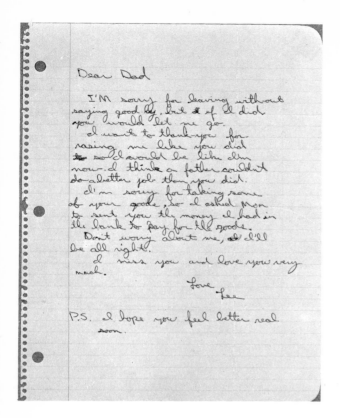

A farewell letter to Dad.

That was a hard question to answer, so we turned into the Molokai Channel outside the harbor. The sea began to be filled with whitecaps. The wind increased from 15 to 25 knots. Art was at the tiller, but as *HIC* bobbed up and down his face turned green and then he was seasick. Suddenly the jib sail ripped along its seam. Jim hoisted a spare sail and *HIC* bounced along over the whitecaps.

Now the heavy dark gray clouds began to roll towards us. We were too far from the breakwater to see that a second red pennant had been raised. Two pennants are a storm warning. Even big yachts do not put to sea when the two red pennants are flying.

As I had had much more sailing experience than Art and Jim, it seemed natural that I should be the boat's skipper. I ordered Jim to furl the mainsail. He had just brought it down when the second jib sail was torn to ribbons. Bits of canvas flew away from the boat. *HIC* was now bare-masted. My main problem was to keep her stern to the sea. The swells were now 20 feet from trough to crest. We were in big trouble. Our hope of surviving was to drift to Lanai Island where we could take our chance with the surf.

Night fell quickly. This was no longer an exciting adventure. The wind gusted at between 30 to 45 knots (about 50 miles an hour). Art was so sick that all he could do was to lie in the bottom of the boat. *HIC* was stronger than she looked and she slithered down the swells, but soon she began to take on water. Every now and then a big comber thudded into the stern. Gallons of water were thrown into the boat.

With two plastic buckets, Jim and I bailed as hard as we could. I could not leave the tiller for long in case *HIC* turned broadside to the swell. If a comber hit us broadside, we would capsize. Nobody could swim in this huge sea.

A storm at night is much more frightening than it is by day. The noise of the wind and the sea was like thunder. It began to get very cold. I was wearing foul-weather clothing, but the spray felt like needles as it hit my face.

The best answer to fear is to keep busy. Fortunately there was little time to think, because when I was not at the tiller I was bailing hard to prevent the boat taking on so much water that she would sink. The bailing helped to keep us from freezing.

If I had allowed myself to think about our danger I might have given up.

Jim had the idea of tying the mainsail across the boat to prevent the water pouring over the side. He tied one end of the sail to the mast and I lashed the other edges to the gunwales. We could just see each other's faces like pale moons. A huge comber hit us and half a ton of water crushed the sail on top of us. Jim and I bailed until our arms ached with pain.

At midnight we heard the sound of an airplane. We did not know it, but the plane was looking for us. We had several flares in a box—the kind of flares used to warn drivers when there is a highway accident. By the time we had managed to light a flare the aircraft was far away.

The sky started to lighten in the east and the storm began to ease up. We hoisted the mainsail, and *HIC* began to move towards Lanai Island. We had not slept at all. Suddenly there was a beautiful sunrise and the sky was absolutely clear. Art switched on our small transistor radio. For a while we listened to music from a Honolulu station. Then the announcer came through with the news. The first news story was:

"The Coast Guard is conducting an extensive air and sea search for three teen-aged boys feared lost at sea. Because of the extreme weather conditions last night, the chances of their survival in a 16-foot boat are very slim."

The report went on to say how we had sailed out of Ala Wai harbor the previous afternoon, and then gave details of our families and school. The station announcer added that the report on the missing teen-aged boys would be updated as further news was received.

How strange it was to be sitting in a boat at sea and to hear our names on the radio! We just looked at each other and then we talked about our parents and how worried they must be. I hoped Mom, still in California, had not heard the news.

We did not know that our adventure was the main news story in all of the Hawaiian newspapers.

Jim, Art and I aboard HIC *in Ala Wai Harbor several days before running away to sea. Photo was taken by our friend, Chuck, in a power boat.*

Teenage trio of adventurers: Art Okkerse, Jim Okkerse, and me.

By sunset that day we managed to sail *HIC* to a cove on Lanai Island. We dropped anchor and waded ashore. We were so tired that we just threw ourselves on the sand and slept. I guess we slept for about three hours. I was awakened by the sound of voices. There was a picnic party a few hundred yards down the beach. We stumbled over the rocks to reach a circle of firelight. The people guessed at once who we were because there had been radio news stories about us all through the day.

One of the people at the picnic drove us to Lanai City and took us to the police station. The police gave us hot coffee and phoned through to Honolulu. Soon we were speaking to our parents. That night Jim, Art and I slept in bunks in jail—not because we were arrested, but because the police saw how badly we needed to sleep. The next day we flew back to Honolulu, leaving our "beat-up" boat to sink in Hulopoe Bay off Manele Beach, Lanai. At the airport we were surrounded by reporters and television cameras. Dad was there. He had been frightened nearly out of his wits for me and was deeply hurt

that I had tried to run away. But of course he was very happy that I wasn't dead.

A few days later, Jim, Art and I had to appear before a Coast Guard inquiry. We were found guilty under a law which prohibits "the reckless operation of a boat, endangering the lives of people." We were told that the air-sea rescue operation had cost $25,000. The Coast Guard court decided not to fine us because, as they said, our parents would have to pay for our foolishness. If we had had to appear in a federal court we could have been sent to a reformatory.

Jim, Art and I were really sorry about the trouble we had caused. But I still longed to sail. Dad thought that I might try to go to sea again.

He said, "Okay, Robin, I'm going to lend you the cash to buy yourself an ocean-going boat. At least I'll know you are reasonably safe. And perhaps you'll learn more from being a sailor than if I sent you to college."

When the school year ended, Dad and I flew back to California where we found a Lapworth sloop in a San Pedro boatyard. She was 24 feet long. Her name was *Dove*.

CHAPTER IV

A Boat Called *Dove*

DOVE WAS five years old but was in good condition. She carried a 30-foot aluminum mast and a 15-foot boom. She drew four feet of water. That meant she could sail in shallow water. Yet she was sturdy enough to sail in big seas.

I was now 16 years old. At first I discussed with Dad just sailing to the South Pacific for a while. Dad had taken a vacation and each day we worked on the boat.

We had to make many changes to get *Dove* ready for ocean sailing. We installed a 30-gallon fresh-water tank—enough fresh water for one person for twelve weeks. Then we put up heavy rigging and fitted the boat with a little kitchen—a kerosene stove sat on a gimbal tray. A gimbal tray is essential for ocean cooking. It stays level and prevents the food from swinging out of the pan whichever way the boat may tip.

We also fitted *Dove* out with a barometer to help me forecast the weather. Reading the barometer is a lot more accurate than reading the clouds.

Another important piece of equipment was the furling gear. This equipment allowed me to raise or lower *Dove's* genoa sail in seconds from the cockpit. When you are sailing alone it is often important to alter the amount of

Dove was a small boat for ocean sailing but we fixed her up with heavy rigging.

sail you carry without having to leave the tiller. A squall can suddenly come out of nowhere. If a squall hits you when you are asleep, a rapid furling can save a boat from losing its mast or having its sails ripped out or something smashed.

We also fixed up a lifeline and harness. I was to wear the harness day and night like a vest. From the harness a nylon rope stretched to the boom. If I fell overboard—not a hard thing to do—I would be able to heave myself back on board.

Other special equipment included a rubber raft, an inflatable one. The pockets in the raft contained bottles of fresh water and some cans of food. If *Dove* sank, at least I would be able to survive for a few days in the rubber raft.

We installed a radio receiver and a chronometer. A chronometer is a ship's clock. It is so accurate that it should not gain or lose more than a second or two a day. If it does lose or gain, it should be always by the same number of seconds. The chronometer and the sextant are used together to find out your exact position at sea.

I had learned how to use the sextant on the voyage to the South Seas. It is an instrument used for measuring the altitude above the horizon of the sun or the moon, or even stars. If you know the height of the sun, say, above the horizon at the exact time, say

With Dad at Hiva Oa, Marquesas

Helping Dad on deck of Valerie

On "Sea Chanty" in Honolulu

30

My early experiences sailing with Dad were preparation for my solo ocean voyage. Dad used his vacation to help me with the new boat; special equipment was installed.

eight o'clock in the morning, you can work out your longitude. You can only find your latitude at noon.

This is where the accuracy of the chronometer is important. If the chronometer is inaccurate by ten seconds, your sun "fix," as it is called, can be wrong by several miles. To help the navigator make proper calculations, there are books issued by the Hydrographic Office. Taking a fix with a sextant sounds quite difficult, but once you know how to do it, it is quite simple. It takes practice, though, like tennis or skiing. Some people spend many years learning how to navigate. I guess I learned to take an accurate fix because I had to.

Also to help my navigation, Dad and I installed a good compass. A sea compass has to be more accurate than the kind you can buy in a supermarket. When you plan to go ocean sailing it is hard to say which piece of equipment is more important than any other. One thing Dad and I had worked on together was how I would sail *Dove* while I was asleep.

We built a self-steering wind vane. The vane is like a small sail at the stern of the boat. This little sail moves a small rudder. The wind vane is really an automatic pilot. I was to find out later that the wind vane was doing a good job, especially if the wind was off the stern quarter or when *Dove* was sailing downwind.

Dad was really clever in making things like this. We had great fun working together at the marina. At night I was tired, but there was still work to be done because I had to study the charts of prevailing winds and currents. I had to learn where the hurricanes

The picture at the right shows the self-steering wind vane that Dad and I installed to act as an automatic pilot whenever I was sleeping. Dad was very clever at making things.

were likely to strike and in addition at what time of the year.

One night, after a long day working on *Dove,* I took my atlas to bed with me to refresh my memory of the islands in the South Pacific. I turned the page to a map of Australia. It did not look so far away.

I turned another page which showed the Indian Ocean. Now supposing, I said to myself, I sailed to Australia, couldn't I sail on into the Indian Ocean and across to Africa—then I could sail through the Suez Canal into the Mediterranean? If I went on sailing westward, I would find myself in the Atlantic Ocean. The Atlantic didn't seem as wide as the Pacific. I could sail through the Panama Canal and arrive back in California. My heart began to thump with excitement.

Dad had not yet gone to bed. He was in the garage working on the gears of *Dove's* wind vane. He looked up when I came in.

"Time you were in bed," he said severely. "We've got a lot of work to do tomorrow."

"Dad," I said, "I've just been looking at my atlas."

"Well?" Dad grunted.

"The world doesn't look all that big," I said.

Dad returned to his workbench. "Is that all you came to tell me?" he asked.

For a moment I just couldn't speak. Then I said, "I was wondering about sailing right around the world."

Dad stopped working. He took off his glasses and wiped them. He put the glasses back on again and then looked at me very hard and with a serious expression.

He said, "The world may look small on your atlas, Robin, but the oceans are not just a piece of paper. When you are out there on those oceans in a sailboat the world is very big indeed."

Dad's glasses seemed to have misted up again. He turned back to his workbench and said gruffly, "Go and get some sleep."

I didn't sleep much that night. Dad hadn't said no. But he hadn't said yes. I guessed he wouldn't say anything more about it until he had talked to Mom. I was sure Mom would say no.

I never did find out what Dad said to Mom, but a few days later, when I was up on *Dove's* mast working on the spreaders, Dad looked up and asked if I wanted any help. I said I was okay.

Dad said, "If you're going to sail around the world, you can't afford to have a loose bolt."

That was it! Dad had agreed to let me try for the biggest sailing adventure of all.

Anybody can talk about sailing around the world. A few people have done it. But I had not heard of any teen-ager who had attempted such a long voyage.

We agreed not to tell anybody about my plan. It would sound like boasting. Most people would think I was crazy. If anything were to go wrong, they would blame my parents for letting me go. We just went on working on *Dove,* making sure that every piece of equipment was as strong and seaworthy as possible. We could take no chances with doing less than that. I had a lot to think about and a lot to do.

The adventure was still like a dream. It was like pretending to sail that boat in the picture of my bedroom when I was eight years old. I felt as if my plan was just something I was imagining—that I would open my eyes and find I was listening to the history teacher, Mr. Caldwell, talking about the signing of the Declaration of Independence, or something.

How long would it take? At first I had thought it might take a year, then 18 months. Then Dad and I figured the voyage would take me two years.

If I had guessed how long the voyage would really take me, I wonder if I would ever have started out.

An atlas is a great book from which to learn the names of places. I checked off the ones I expected to visit. In my imagination I was already on my way. Distances do not seem so far on a map but I was to discover a difference.

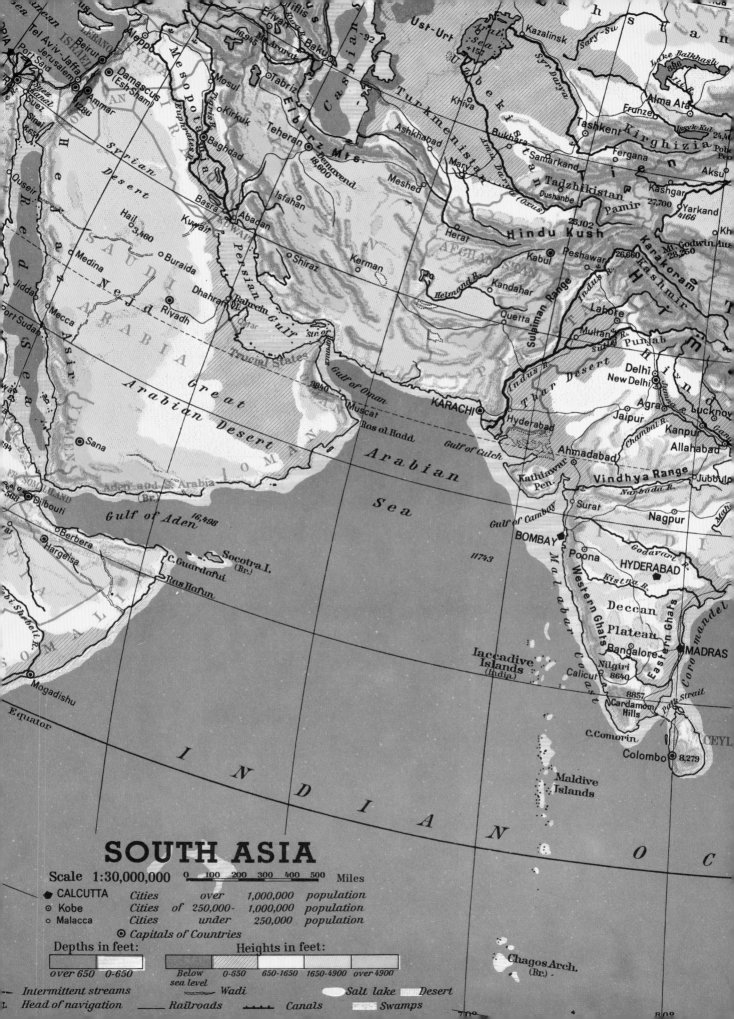

SOUTH ASIA

Scale 1:30,000,000

0   100   200   300   400   500   Miles

- ● CALCUTTA   *Cities*   *over*   1,000,000   *population*
- ◉ Kobe   *Cities of* 250,000-   1,000,000   *population*
- ○ Malacca   *Cities*   *under*   250,000   *population*
- ◉ *Capitals of Countries*

Depths in feet: **Heights in feet:**

over 650   0-650   Below   0-650   650-1650   1650-4900   over 4900
                          sea level

- -- *Intermittent streams*   ─ *Wadi*   *Salt lake*   *Desert*
- *Head of navigation*   ─ *Railroads*   ···· *Canals*   *Swamps*

CHAPTER V

Starting the Voyage

It was a beautiful morning on July 27, 1965. *Dove* was tied up at the marina at San Pedro, a fishing port near Long Beach and one of the entrances to the Port of Los Angeles.

Somehow my secret had got out. Anyway, the television and radio people and newspaper reporters were at the marina waiting for me. I was really embarrassed because I had not done anything. The reporters asked lots of questions, like why was I doing it? and how did I manage to get my parents' permission? and would I still be doing my schoolwork? and wasn't I scared?

Two school friends, Jud Croft and Jill Gibson, had come up from Newport Beach. Dad was there, of course. It wasn't easy for him. He knew that if anything went wrong on my voyage, many people would blame him. In fact, plenty of people blamed him already for "letting his son commit suicide," as a letter in one newspaper had put it.

Mom was now in Hawaii setting up our new home. I hoped to be seeing her within a month because Hawaii would be my first port of call.

Uncle Dick arrived with a basket which he handed over to me. I had thought the present was fruit or candy, but when I looked inside the basket two small kittens popped out. I named the kittens Joliette and Suzette

Inside the basket were two small kittens.

for the two Polynesian girls who had been offered to my parents as a trade for me three years earlier. The kittens had been born in a closet. They became quite famous because pictures of them were printed in newspapers and magazines all over the world.

Dad came aboard and shook my hand. It was hard for both of us to say anything, but Dad said, "Good luck, son—I will see you in Hawaii."

At 10 o'clock, with the mist lifting off the outer harbor, I started up *Dove's* inboard engine.

My voyage around the world had begun.

The excitement of starting lasted all through my first day at sea. I tuned into my favorite Los Angeles music station and heard the announcer interrupt the music to report that "schoolboy Robin Lee Graham has just set off from San Pedro on his lone global voyage." He added, "The most important piece of Robin's luggage is a box full of schoolbooks."

I did have my schoolbooks with me but I didn't think of them being more important than my compass, sextant and barometer. The books were tucked away under old clothing which I had bought at a church sale and at a flea market. My idea was to exchange the old clothing for food when I reached the islands. Also for trading, I had taken aboard four hundred ballpoint pens.

In my billfold I had forty dollars. That was not much for a global voyage. As a farewell present Dad had given me a small battery-driven tape recorder. Dad knew I was pretty bad at writing letters. I promised to send the tapes back home as a sort of diary.

At first the kittens seemed to enjoy sailing, but when *Dove* passed the breakwater at the entrance to the harbor the swell began to increase. Then the kittens were seasick. As the sun went down and the lights of Catalina Island began to fade, I felt sick too.

But my sickness was loneliness. I thought of turning back. Then I began to think what everyone would say if my attempt to sail around the world lasted only one day. That thought kept me sailing westwards.

I turned on my new tape recorder and spoke into the microphone. I said, "The kittens are wet with spray. I have just dried them off and now they have taken over my sleeping bag. Catalina is almost out of sight.

The wind is a steady 15 knots. Gee, I feel lonely out here."

I flicked on the port and starboard lights. The port light is red and the starboard light is green. It is the law of the sea that these lights must be lit at sundown. I also lit up a very bright kerosene Coleman lamp suspended over the cockpit. The Coleman flooded the sails with light to give warning to shipping that might be in my path.

The Coleman had to be pumped up every two hours. This meant that I was not able to sleep right through the night.

At nine o'clock on my first night at sea I made my first meal. I just heated up a can of stew on the gimballed stove. I gave the kittens some fresh milk and sardines which they immediately threw up.

Then I sat under the Coleman in the cockpit feeling sorry for myself. How crazy can I be, I thought. The whole idea of trying to sail around the world was just mad. If I was

My Coleman lamp brightened the dark but not my spirit.

lonely now, what would I feel like in the middle of the Pacific?

But the beauty of the night helped to take my mind off my loneliness. The sea was lit by phosphorescence—tiny flashlights in the wake of *Dove*. The phosphorescence comes from small living sea creatures. The little lights reminded me of looking down on Los Angeles from an airplane at night.

Then above me the stars twinkled. When you look at the stars from a city, it is like looking through a dirty window. The smog and the city lights take the brilliance out of the heavens. But at sea, where the air is clear and there is no glare, the stars become as brilliant as diamonds on black velvet.

I never lost my excitement at looking at the stars. I was able to pick out the important ones. Soon I was to learn how to navigate by the moon and stars as easily as I could navigate by the sun.

I began to think about how big the universe is and how the light from some of the stars started out toward the earth thousands and thousands of years ago.

But I was lonelier than I had ever been before. Loneliness was like a bad toothache. I thought it would go away as soon as I had gotten used to it. But it never did go away for long. We are so used to having people about us, to hearing the sounds of voices, the traffic and things like that. So when there is absolute silence, when you know that there is nobody within shouting distance, the silence can make you crazy—almost.

I didn't sleep that first night. For one thing I worried that in the busy shipping lane near Los Angeles a big ship would not see *Dove's* lights and would run me down. But when the sky started to lighten in the east I went to sleep. I had to push Joliette and Suzette out of my sleeping bag. They snuggled up on my pillow. It is pretty hard to sleep when you have the whiskers of two little kittens tickling your face.

When I awakened, I checked the compass and was pleased to see that the self-steering wind vane had kept *Dove* right on course.

My early training with a sextant was a necessity in preparing for my sea voyage. I knew exactly where I was.

I took a sun fix with the sextant, and then worked out my position. I knew exactly where I was, even though I could not see any land. I then entered my position in *Dove's* logbook.

Every ocean-going ship has a logbook. It is really a ship's diary. My logbook was a green cashbook. On the cover I wrote, "Logbook of Yacht *Dove* by Captain R. L. Graham." My first entry read, "Left San Pedro July 27, 1965. Time, 1100 hours. Total miles 0." My entry on the second day read, "Time 1000 hours. Miles 117." This meant that in 23 hours I had traveled a satisfactory distance.

37

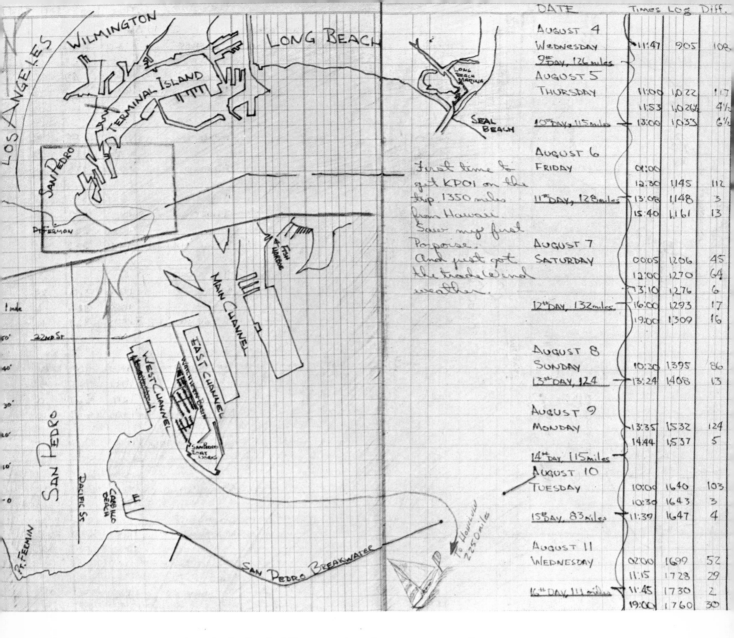

An early entry in Dove's *logbook. The captain of every ocean-going vessel keeps a record of the distance traveled and of unusual events.*

Besides finding my latitude from noon fixes, there was another way of checking my mileage. I had a taffrail log-spinner trailing out astern of *Dove*. This works like an automobile's mileage clock. As the boat travels through the water, a little free-running propeller spins with the movement of the water. The propeller turns a thin cable attached to a dial on the stern rail. It tells you how much water you have traveled through by the number of revolutions the propeller has made. With the taffrail log-spinner I could tell how fast *Dove* was moving over the wa-

ter. This reading is not always a test of speed because currents can make a difference. If you are traveling with the current—and some currents have a speed of several miles an hour—then the boat can actually be moving much faster "over the bottom" than the taffrail log-spinner indicates.

By getting a sun fix with the sextant and by checking the taffrail log-spinner, I could tell within a few miles the distance I had traveled.

So I could guess how long it would take me to reach Hawaii if the wind remained steady. The prevailing wind was about 15 knots off the port beam. I figured it would take three weeks to make Honolulu.

I sure was looking forward to Honolulu because Dad would be there. Dad was planning to fly to Hawaii as soon as I had left San Pedro.

One of my friends is an airline pilot. He once told me that flying an airliner is almost as easy as riding a bike once you know how to read your instruments. But pilots are trained for emergencies that may never happen—the times when all the instrument panel lights start blinking red.

Ocean sailing is like this. Any kid can quickly learn to sail a boat. What I still had to find out was whether I was able to handle an emergency situation. I was to find this out before long.

Here I am in Dove's *cabin making notations in my logbook. I am wearing a safety harness. The map below shows the first landfall.*

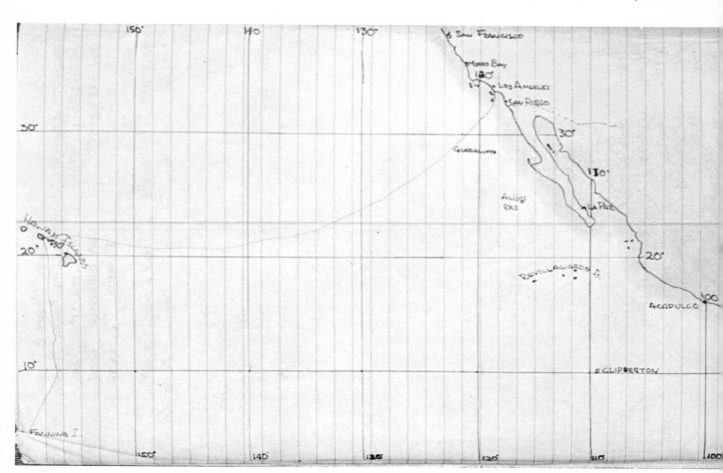

CHAPTER VI

The First Port

THE VOYAGE to Hawaii was easy sailing. Most of the time I hardly had to alter the sails. Occasionally the wind was strong enough for the gunwales to dip under the water.

Joliette and Suzette soon found their sea legs. They loved to watch the water streaming past. The two kittens sat on the top of the cabin and tried to paw at the moving water as if they were playing with a mouse. They soon learned that it was not much good trying to catch water. All they got were wet paws.

A good thing about cats is that they are so clean. They almost always used the litter box and hardly ever messed up the deck. They were careful not to walk too close to the side of the boat, even when they were chasing each other around the deck.

I was a bad cook. I had thought that cooking would be easy, but my meals usually tasted awful. On my third night I spoke into the tape recorder and said, "Just had a dinner of turkey and yams which stuck to the roof of my mouth. I'll just have to do something about my cooking." A day later I recorded, "Why is my rice always so soggy? I wish I had learned something about cooking from Mom."

On the tenth day out from San Pedro, *Dove* hit the trade winds. These are welcome winds for a sailor. They really push a boat along at a good clip.

I still found it best to sleep in the early morning and in the afternoon and then to stay awake at night and keep a lookout for lights on the horizon. Sometimes I read in the light of the Coleman lamp, but mostly I just sat there in the cockpit thinking about things. On my tenth night at sea the moon was so bright that I was able to see the horizon clearly, and this allowed me to take my first star fix with the sextant. I told my tape recorder, "It's the middle of the night and I know exactly where I am—and that's kind of fun."

I thought how fascinating it was that the sun and the moon and the stars keep much better time than any man-made clock or watch. America has a master clock at the National Observatory in Washington, D.C. But this master clock has to be corrected occasionally by checking it against the master clock of the universe.

When I was about halfway between Hawaii and Los Angeles, I wrote a note and put it into a bottle. The note read, "My name is Robin Lee Graham. I am 16 years old and I am sailing a 24-foot sailboat. My position is 127 degrees West and 22 degrees North. Please, if you find this note, write to me and

At Honolulu, my first landfall, I was given a necklace of flowers. This old Hawaiian custom is an invitation to return.

tell me where you found it. Thanks a lot." I gave my uncle's address in Los Angeles.

I watched the bottle bob along in the wake of *Dove*. Perhaps it is still floating about in the Pacific, because nobody has written to me to say that they have found it.

There was always something to do, like washing down the deck or cleaning up the cabin. The cabin always needed tidying up. The only scary thing that happened was when I suddenly noticed water sloshing about under my feet. I thought *Dove* had sprung a leak and was sinking. I was about to blow up my rubber life raft when I found out the trouble. One of the small plastic fittings below the waterline had fallen out.

The plug was near the exhaust pipe of the inboard engine. The heat from the engine, which I used to charge the batteries, had melted it. Anyway, I had to do something quickly. I made another plug out of wood and pumped the water out of the bilge. Safe again! Wow, that was scary!

On my 16th day at sea, my radio picked up Hawaiian music. I thought the cats would be as excited as I was, but they went on chasing each other's tails.

Joliette and Suzette were more excited when the first flying fish landed on the deck. These fish don't really fly, but it seems as if they do. When they are out of the water they push out their fins and sort of glide for

A flying fish landed on the deck causing a great deal of excitement.
Joliette and Suzette finished him off quickly.

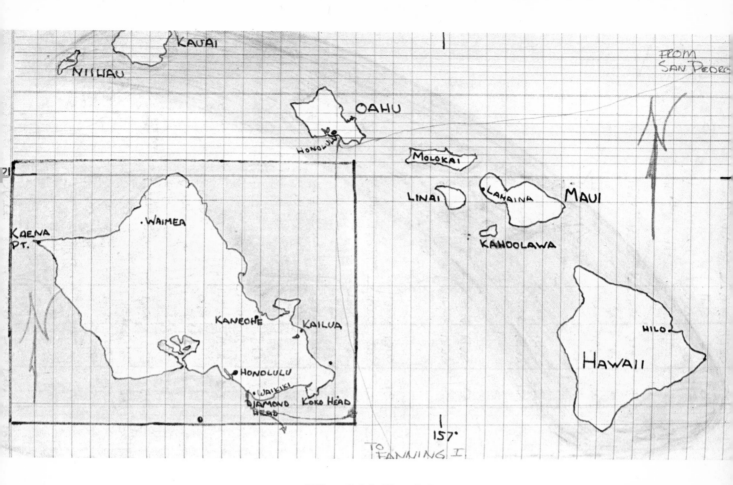

When I left Honolulu to sail south to tiny Fanning Island,
my father said, "Robin, you are moving into the big league."
It was difficult to leave; I was homesick already.

quite a distance. The little flying fish must have thought *Dove* was a whale or a shark and they wanted to get out of the way quickly. The kittens raced me to the foredeck and pounced on the fish. They were proud of their first catch and really enjoyed it. After they had eaten even the bones, they licked their paws and purred.

My own first attempt to catch a fish was not successful. I thought it would be fun to try to shoot a fish with a bow and arrow. I filled a plastic bag with some sardines and let the bag float behind *Dove* on a piece of string. I held the other end of the string in my teeth so that I would be able to use both hands to shoot the arrow. Sure enough, a mahimahi (dolphin) I had seen cruising around the boat came to the surface and sniffed the sardines. I pulled back the bow

and aimed. The fish struck so hard that it nearly pulled out my front teeth. I never tried fishing with my teeth again!

"Land!" I shouted.

It was my 22nd day at sea, and I had raised the island of Oahu. I whooped with joy. Joliette and Suzette arched their backs. That evening I was outside Ala Wai harbor at Honolulu. The radio and television stations had been talking about me, so there were several small boats to give me a welcome. A reporter told me I was the youngest sailor to have sailed alone from mainland America to Hawaii.

But I was much more excited to see my parents. This was a very different Hawaiian reception from the time when Jim, Art and I had returned to Honolulu from our ill-fated voyage in *HIC*.

CHAPTER VII

Cheerful Visitors

ON SEPTEMBER 14, I was ready to sail again. In a way the voyage to Hawaii had been a shakedown cruise—a chance to make sure that *Dove* was in good condition.

Now Dad warned me, "Robin, you are moving into the big league." He meant that the next stage of the voyage would really test my sailing skills.

Again, there were many newspaper reporters and television people at the yacht basin when I stepped aboard *Dove*. I was glad Mom was wearing dark glasses because I knew she was crying.

It was much harder to say goodbye this time. But everyone else was cheerful. Following the island custom, my friends put flower leis around my neck. They were wreaths made from frangipani flowers with a beautiful scent. Tiny leis were put around the necks of Joliette and Suzette. Hawaiians say that if you throw the leis into the sea when you leave the islands, you will return.

As soon as I had sailed *Dove* out of the harbor I threw my leis into the water, but I forgot to throw away the leis which circled the necks of the kittens like flea collars. The kittens were never to return to Hawaii.

The wind died almost as soon as I got out of the harbor. I was not as cheerful as I pretended to be. My throat was so tight I could hardly swallow a drink of root beer.

I told the tape recorder: "Sure hated to leave. I wonder if I will ever see my parents again. I suppose saying goodbye always hurts, but it can't hurt more than this. Kittens look miserable too. Gee, I'm homesick!"

I wasn't at all hungry, but I had to do something to stop myself from crying. As I looked at the lights of Honolulu fading into the distance, I made a canned spaghetti dinner.

Suddenly a squall raced down on *Dove*. I was soon sailing through pelting rain and high wind and had to drop the mainsail. I furled the genoa too, so as to prevent *Dove* from capsizing.

The storm was the best thing that could have happened to me on my first night at sea. It kept me so busy that I had no time to feel sorry for myself.

Before leaving Honolulu I had worked out my course. I planned to sail almost due south to the tiny island of Fanning, just a speck on the map 1,000 miles away. If *Dove* made 100 miles a day, I should be at Fanning in ten days.

Four days out of Honolulu the color of the water changed to a really beautiful clear blue. I was tempted to jump over the side and take a swim. Although I was wearing a safety harness, it would have been crazy to swim. A sudden puff of wind could have pushed *Dove* along at six knots. At that speed it would have been difficult if not impossible to haul myself back on board again.

Besides, there were sharks about. I had not yet seen a shark, but I knew they were around. They were real man-eaters.

Twelve days out of Honolulu *Dove* hit the doldrums. The sails just flopped about. Every now and then a gentle puff would nudge *Dove* on her way, but in one 24-hour period we made only 27 miles. If I had been in a rowboat I could have gone farther.

That evening I was very depressed. Joliette and Suzette were flopped out in the heat. To make them more comfortable I dipped towels in the sea and wrapped the damp cloths around the kittens. The three of us were really miserable when suddenly I heard a noise I had not heard before. Joliette and Suzette pricked up their ears.

We had visitors! Porpoises were swimming and diving about *Dove*. I turned on my tape recorder and this is what I said:

"They are all around us now, these happy porpoises. Listen! Can you hear them talking? It's amazing how loud they squeak. Thump! Did you hear that! One of the porpoises bumped against *Dove's* keel. It's really exciting. It's been so long since I've heard a human voice and now it's almost as though someone was trying to speak to me."

No creature has a happier face than a porpoise. He's always smiling and seems to be having lots of fun. It seemed as though these porpoises had just come over to *Dove* to cheer me up.

After splashing about *Dove* for about ten minutes, the porpoises suddenly swam away. How much better I felt!

A friendly porpoise took away my loneliness; he almost seemed to speak.

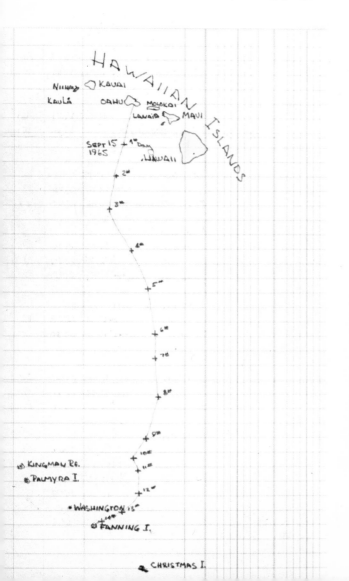

CHAPTER VIII

A Broken Wing

IN THE MIDDLE of the Pacific I knew there was only the smallest chance of *Dove* having a collision with another boat. In fact, I had not seen any boats at all since leaving Honolulu. It was safe to sleep at night.

Even when asleep I could hear if there was any change in the wind or in the movement of the sea. Then I would wake up at once and check my compass and sails. One night I heard a change of wave patterns while I was asleep. I jumped out of my bunk and went to the cockpit. Nothing seemed to be wrong. Then I looked at the compass. Instead of sailing south I was sailing due north—back to Honolulu! For the first time my automatic pilot had not worked. *Dove* had swung right around. I pushed over the rudder and *Dove* was again on her way to Fanning Island.

Joliette and Suzette were good company. I often talked to them as if they were human beings. I said dumb things, like "Okay, Joliette, what shall we have for breakfast? Hot cereal today? Well, I'll give you hot cereal if you will help me wash the dishes."

Of course the cats never answered me. Sometimes they would mew and purr, but mostly they just jumped about the deck or snuggled up on my bunk or slipped into my sleeping bag.

I tried my skill at climbing a coconut tree. Fanning's main crop is copra.

When I figured I was getting close to Fanning Island I really became nervous. Although Fanning was a few miles across, I could easily miss the island altogether if my sextant readings were wrong or if my chronometer was just a few seconds out.

Then suddenly I saw it—just a tiny little smudge on the horizon.

Joliette and Suzette had no idea why I was so excited. They stared at me as if I had gone completely crazy.

In the late afternoon I sailed close to the island, which was dark green with tropical trees and shrubs. Then I saw a power boat coming toward me. A white man wearing a peaked cap shouted, "Hullo." Except for hearing myself and the radio, this was the first human voice I had heard in two weeks.

The man threw me a rope and towed *Dove* into the harbor. We tied up at a stone jetty. I climbed up the steps and the man put out his hand. "Welcome to Fanning," he said. "We don't get many visitors here. My name's Philip Palmer. Who are you?"

"Robin Graham," I said. I wanted to tell him a lot of things, but I found that my tongue would not catch up to my thoughts. If you don't converse for a long time you forget how to speak. I felt pretty silly.

Mr. Palmer invited me to his little cottage to have dinner. He was the boss of the island. Fanning's main crop is copra. This is the dried kernel of the coconut from which coconut oil is made. About 300 natives from the Gilbert Islands harvested the crop. The workers had their wives and children with them, and they spoke a language I could not understand.

It was nice to sit down to a real meal again. Mr. Palmer's housekeeper, Marybell, made a special dinner of fresh fish and rice. Fish were so easy to catch, I could have almost hooked them on my toenails.

I visited the island's school. The children sang a special song for me in their Gilbertine language. For a time they were shy and stared at me as if I had come from the moon. I was the only white boy they had ever seen.

I grinned at the children and they grinned back. Then they asked me to dance with them. It was a pretty wild dance, to the rhythm of a drum. Although we couldn't speak each other's language, we laughed a lot and made signs with our hands.

On Sunday the children took me to their little church and prayed for me in their own language. Mr. Palmer translated for me. The children prayed that I would travel safely in my little boat.

It was hard to leave these happy people. Before I left I gave a Mickey Mouse shirt to Marybell's little boy, who was sick. He seemed pleased, although I could see he did not know who Mickey Mouse was. But he thought that an animal with big black ears and wearing a pair of pants was very funny.

Marybell and Mr. Palmer gave me some fresh eggs and bread made with coconut

Dove anchored peacefully off Fanning Island.

KINGMAN RF.

LINE ISLANDS

.PALMYRA

WASHINGTON○

FANNING ○
OCT.5
1965 +1st DAY

+2nd

○ JARVIS I.

+3rd

+4th

PHOENIX Is.

•ENDERBURY

NIE• •PHOENIX

+5th

' SYDNEY

+6th

+7th

+8th •WAIRUNA
PD (2ND 1915)

+9th

+10th

ATAFU

•NUKUNONO

•FAKOFO

+11th

RAKAHANGA •

• MANIHIKI

DISCOL'D WATER
(RED 1926)

+12th

• DANGER I.
○ TEMA RF.

• NASSAU I

• SWAIN I

+13th

+14th

○ SAVAROV I

+16th +15th

TUTUILA○ MANUA Is.
○

• ROSE I.

SAMOA ISLANDS

LEFT ~~HONOLULU~~ FANNING   OCTOBER 4
AT 12'00 NOON   MONDAY   12:00 065   36³
                  1st DAY, 59 miles

                  OCT.   5
                  TUESDAY   09:45 120   55 372
                                   12:10 124   4 372
                  2nd DAY, 85 miles 12:31 124   0 372

                  OCT.   6
                  WEDNESDAY   08:50 191   67 379
                  3rd DAY, 122 miles 12:30 209   18 380

                  OCT.   7
                  THURSDAY   08:55 314 105 391⁴
CROSSED THE EQUATOR   12:34 331   17 393¹
AT   10:30 OCT.7.65
                  4th DAY, 110 miles
                  OCT.   8
                  FRIDAY   09:45 427   96 402
CHANGED TO   11:38 441   14 404
ZONE +11   5th DAY, 90 miles
                  OCT   9
                  SATURDAY   08:50 523   82 412
                                   11:39 531   8 413

                  6th DAY, 43 miles
                  OCT   10
                  SUNDAY   08:20 565   34 416⁹
                  7th DAY, 31 miles 11:35 574   9 417⁴

                  OCT.   11
                  MONDAY   09:30 605   31 420
ABOUT 12:00 TODAY A SHARK ATE   11:41 605   0 420
THE ROTARY OF MY TAFF RAIL LOG.   12:00

                  8th DAY, 42 miles ?

In this entry of my logbook, I recorded crossing the equator. Joliette and Suzette officially become "shellbacks."

milk. They also gave me a hand-carved model canoe. They would not take any money. In fact, my visit to Fanning Island cost me exactly twenty cents—one dime and two nickels which had fallen out of my pocket at the dance. One of the children found the three coins and came running down to *Dove* to return them to me. That kind of honesty is pretty rare in most places. I told the small boy he could keep the money. He was so pleased you'd have thought he had become a millionaire.

When I put out to sea again I felt really homesick—this time for simple island people who had quickly become my friends.

Before leaving Fanning I sent a cablegram to my parents, but it never arrived. Back in Hawaii, I learned later, they were very worried about me. The newspapers in Hawaii and in California had big headlines reading, "BOY SAILOR IS MISSING" and "NO WORD FROM ROBIN GRAHAM!"

Meanwhile I sailed "wing and wing" towards my next port of call, Pago Pago (pronounced Pango Pango). When a yacht sails wing and wing, the mainsail is out on the one side of the boat and a jib or genoa sail is out on the other. When you see a yacht sailing wing and wing, it looks like a big butterfly. You can only sail like this

"Wing and wing," we crossed the equator; it was so hot that I wanted to jump overboard to swim, but there were too many sharks about.

when the wind is at your back. One advantage of sailing wing and wing is that the boat has a nicer motion. It is also fast sailing.

I began to study my schoolbooks and finished part one of my American literature course by reading the lives of Captain John Smith and Benjamin Franklin. It was much nicer doing schoolwork in a boat than in a classroom! There was plenty of time, too, because soon *Dove* struck the doldrums again. She just wallowed about in the water. It began to get very hot. On October 7 I took a sextant reading and figured I was crossing the equator. I wrote in my logbook, "Joliette and Suzette are officially shellbacks." This is the name sailors give to anyone who has crossed the equator.

At one point I really thought I had gone crazy. A friend in Honolulu had given me a cup and ball game which I had placed on a shelf in the cabin. I was fixing up my bunk

when I saw that the cup and ball were under my pillow. I couldn't figure out how they had gotten there and I put the game back on the shelf. Then I had to do something on the deck, but ten minutes later when I returned to the cabin the cup and ball were half hidden under my pillow.

I got really scared. What was happening to my mind? Anyway, I put the game back on the shelf once more and returned to deck. Then I heard a slight thump and jumped back into the cabin. It was Suzette. She was pulling the cup and ball off the shelf and trying to hide them under my pillow.

Because I was so pleased that I had not gone crazy, I didn't punish Suzette. But when she started to hide my Fanning Island eggs I had to teach her a lesson.

The cats were always looking for something to play with—anything which moved, even the shadow of a rope.

My slow progress across the doldrums was really getting me down. I burst into tears just because a rice pudding I had tried to make had failed to turn out properly. The rice was as tough as a bicycle tire.

I happen to hate sharks. I saw a five-foot man-eater swimming around *Dove* and I fired a shot. The shark turned over and disappeared. Then I saw the cable to the taffrail log-spinner was floating on the top of the water. The shark had bitten right through the line. Guess what would have happened if I had been dangling a leg over the side! Anyway, now I had to estimate the distance each day without help from my taffrail log-spinner.

Fifteen days out of Fanning I spotted land. I had raised Tutuila, the main island of American Samoa. I told the cats how lucky they were to have such a good navigator.

"Pride comes before a fall," my mother used to say. It sure worked out that way with me. Suddenly a squall hit *Dove,* and a stay (one of the steel ropes holding up the mast) snapped. The mast fell into the sea, dragging the sails with it.

Dove stopped like a bird full of buckshot. It took 20 minutes to heave sodden sails and the broken mast back to the deck, and another two hours to lift up the boom and give *Dove* a "jury rig," or temporary rigging.

The boom was now my stubby mainmast and I fixed the mainsail to it. *Dove* now looked more like the little dinghy I had sailed at Morro Bay. The problem with jury rigging is that it makes a boat difficult to control. Although Tutuila was only 15 miles away, the wind was on the wrong quarter. I could only sail downwind. This meant that I could not sail to Tutuila. I looked at my charts and figured that I would have to sail for Apia on Upolu Island in British Samoa.

Upolu was 50 miles away and the island's shoreline was treacherous with hidden reefs and pounding surf. Night was falling. *Dove* had a broken wing.

This would be the first big test of my seamanship.

A shark is no friendly visitor. Dove *survived a hurricane in Tutuila.*

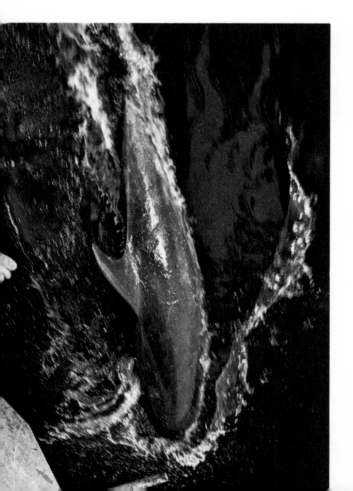
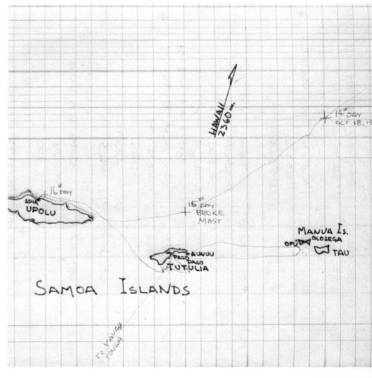

CHAPTER IX

Tellers of Tales

IT WAS a long night. I could hear the surf pounding the rocks a few hundred yards away. With a change in the wind, *Dove* could be wrecked.

The sun rose and illuminated golden beaches and beautiful green hills. At noon I sailed crippled *Dove* into Apia harbor.

The first thing I saw was the wreck of a German warship which had been sunk by a hurricane. If a hurricane could do that to a big warship, I hated to think what a hurricane could do to little *Dove*.

After I had thrown out an anchor, two small boys paddled up to *Dove*.

"Me dive for pennies," they shouted.

I threw some cents into the water and the boys dived and collected them before they hit the bottom.

The boys laughed, their teeth shining like pearls. They wanted to know where I had come from. I told them I had come from America.

"Where your crew?" asked one of the boys.

"No crew," I said.

"You eat crew?" asked the boys. They laughed so much they nearly fell out of their canoe.

After I had reached the harbor and had cleared my papers with the customs officials,

A distress signal goes up
after a treacherous pounding.

the boys took me down Apia's main street. I said I was hungry, so they took me to Aggie's Hotel.

Aggie's Hotel is quite famous. It was built by Aggie Grey, whose father was a New Zealander and whose mother was a Polynesian. The boys introduced me to Aggie, whose hair was white. She looked me up and down and then said, "Oh, I know who you are. You are Robin Lee Graham, the schoolboy sailor."

I looked surprised, so she explained that she had read about me in some American newspapers.

Aggie showed me the headlines saying that I was feared lost at sea. I immediately ran to the post office and sent a cable to Mom and Dad in Hawaii.

Aggie was really kind. She said I could have meals at her hotel whenever I wanted to, and that she would not charge me anything. Her son, Alan, took me to a teacher at the technical school who "could fix anything." The teacher, Mr. Heywood, mended *Dove's* mast.

Then I visited the grave of the famous author, Robert Louis Stevenson, who had died on the island. I had read one of Stevenson's books, *Treasure Island*. He was one of my favorite authors and I was interested to see where he had been buried.

The island people had loved the Scots author so much that they had built a road to

Tomb of Robert Louis Stevenson, "Teller of Tales."

his grave. They called it "The Road of Loving Hearts." They had given the author a special name which means "Teller of Tales."

Carved into the tomb were the words:

> *Home is the sailor, home from the sea,*
> *And the Hunter home from the hill.*

An islander gave me an outrigger canoe, so each day I paddled to and from *Dove*. I didn't allow Joliette and Suzette to go ashore for fear they would get lost.

One night when I was sleeping aboard *Dove*, I heard Joliette crying. I went up on deck and discovered that Suzette had fallen into the water and was thrashing about. I scooped up Suzette and dried her down. If Joliette had not cried for her friend, Suzette would have been drowned.

Because this was the hurricane season and because I was waiting for new rigging to arrive from America, I was not ready to sail again for a while. I spent Christmas in Apia and exchanged presents with Aggie and my new friends. Mom and Dad sent me a spare plastic sextant, more tapes for my recorder, a new taffrail log-spinner and a Gibson Girl radio transmitter. The Gibson Girl transmitter was invented in World War II and could send out distress signals.

At Apia I enjoyed sitting down with the islanders and listening to their stories. They had stories about everything. One old man told me the legend of the coconut tree. He spoke English quite well.

Once upon a time, he said, there was a girl called Sina who was the most beautiful girl in all the islands. A king decided to marry Sina, but as he didn't want to frighten her he disguised himself as an eel. The eel became Sina's special pet, but when the eel tried to kiss Sina the girl got frightened and fled from island to island. The eel-king chased her until he was tired and dying. With his last

54

breath he explained to Sina that he was really a king and that he loved her. He pleaded with Sina to bury him in front of her hut. She promised she would. Sina fulfilled her promise and later she watched an eel-like plant growing out of the ground. It grew into a beautiful, tall tree. This was the first coconut tree. Every time Sina took a drink of coconut milk she knew she was kissing the king who had loved her so much.

The islanders told many fables like this. I guess the stories had been told by parents to their children for hundreds of years.

Another friend, George, invited me to climb Mount Matavanu on the nearby island of Savaii. Some children in the village below the mountain said that it was haunted and that that was why the islanders never climbed it.

George and I were near the mountain peak when it grew dark. We made beds of ferns and tried to sleep. The silence was weird. It was easy to imagine that spooks were walking about. I didn't get much sleep.

Next morning, when we climbed down the mountain we were thirsty. George knew what to do. He cut a vine with his bush knife and a few seconds later the vine whistled like a boiling kettle and liquid poured out of it. I was surprised to find the drink almost as refreshing as Kool-Aid.

The children in the village thought we were lost or had been caught by the ghosts. They came up to meet us and guided us back to the village. I was so grateful that I gave them my tennis shoes, a bush knife and my spare pair of Levi's.

By January, *Dove* was ready for sea again. I said goodbye to Aggie and Alan and to my other friends and sailed out of the harbor towards neighboring Pago Pago.

Some porpoises came up to *Dove* and squeaked at me. They seemed to say, "Welcome back to the sea again."

A few hours' sailing brought us to Pago Pago harbor, where other yachts joined us during a hurricane.

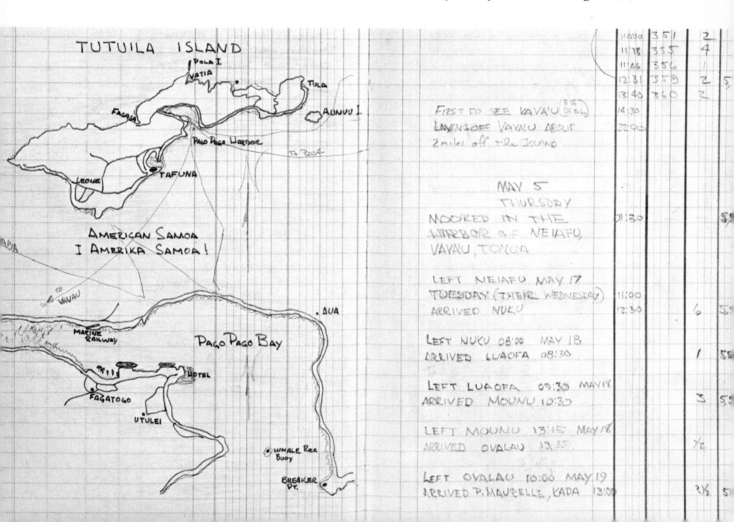

CHAPTER X

Hurricane!

IT WAS still the hurricane season, so I had to be careful. I thought it best to stay at Pago Pago for a while.

My school friend Jud Croft flew out from California. I was glad to have his company. One afternoon *Dove* was swinging from a buoy in Pago Pago harbor when a Coast Guard boat came alongside. An officer shouted through a bullhorn that we should "batten down" as a hurricane was on the way. Jud and I tied everything down and we took off *Dove's* sails. We also put out more mooring lines.

The barometer fell from 29.70 to 29.20 in three hours. I had never known the barometer to fall so rapidly. The sunset looked real ugly. Two big ocean-going yachts scuttled into the harbor. Jud and I felt pretty snug in *Dove's* cabin. Through the porthole I could see the swell being whipped into whitecaps. Before night fell, the wind carried the spray off the top of the whitecaps and hurled it across the top of the sea. It was like being in a snowstorm.

I turned on my little tape recorder and gave a running commentary of the great storm. This is what I reported:

"Outside it is like a blizzard because the wind is whipping the spray against the portholes. Now *Dove* is rolling from gunwale to gunwale. . . ."

At ten o'clock I told my tape recorder, "Never imagined there could be wind like this. Through the portholes I can see the lights of the town going out. Whole streets are suddenly going dark as the power fails. The radio says the full force of the hurricane won't hit us until about midnight. Boy, here we go! Hold on! Wow! That blast of wind dipped the port gunwale right under water. This is really exciting. Jud and I are just laughing and shouting down here in the cabin." We were enjoying the whole thing.

At midnight I reported, "The noise is now unbelievable. Radio says winds are more than a hundred miles an hour . . . *Dove*—. . . no, I can't believe it! . . . The wind is picking up *Dove* and throwing her on her side until the portholes are covered with water. Imagine that! No sails, just bare poles. But the sea is pouring over the cockpit combing. This is really swinging, man! The portholes have again just gone right under water. . . . Boy, my ears are popping . . . Suzette and Joliette are keeping their cool. I guess they know that cats have nine lives . . . There are still some lights on in the harbor, and I can just make out palm trees kissing the ground . . . Look out! I thought we had had it then! We just heeled over at 85 degrees . . ."

Jud and I were so excited that we forgot to be frightened. We laughed and yelled as if we were on a roller-coaster.

I was excited by the hurricane, but many homes were damaged.

Many Samoan homes are built of grass and are quickly destroyed in a storm.

If I had been sailing on the ocean instead of being anchored in Pago Pago harbor, I would not now be telling this story. One yacht, the *Marinero,* with a crew of three was sailing somewhere west of Samoa. I had gotten to know the three young men who were sailing her. Several days after the hurricane the Coast Guard picked up bits and pieces of the *Marinero.* They never found the bodies of my friends.

The hurricane died as quickly as it had come. Next morning Jud and I looked for damage to *Dove.* The only harm she had suffered was to a small section of the jib sail. It had torn loose from the lashing and had been shredded into string.

The island was in an awful mess. Jud and I hitched a ride to the village of Tula, which had taken the full force of the storm. Most of the islanders' houses had been blown away.

Samoans usually build their homes out of cane and matting. Although the houses are easily destroyed, they are easy to rebuild. By the time we arrived at Tula the people were already busy rebuilding their homes. Jud and I wanted to help lift fallen trees which were blocking the roads. The people were so happy to see us that they didn't want us to work at all. We were happy too.

A Polynesian lady, Mrs. Fa'av Pritchard, who lived in one of the few concrete homes, invited us to spend the night with her family. Everybody was talking about the great hurricane and how lucky they were to have escaped with their lives.

Mrs. Pritchard asked me what I was doing on the island. I told her about *Dove* and how I hoped to sail around the world. She looked at me a long time without saying anything. Then she said, "I'm going to give you an island name. You are now 'Lupe Lele.' In our language that means 'Flying Dove.' May the wind take you safely to where you want to go." I gave her a kiss.

That night Mrs. Pritchard made us a supper of banana pancakes. They were really good. Many of the village people came in to talk to us about America. Everybody had a good meal and a good time. We sang songs and danced. One old lady, whose face was as wrinkled as a walnut, danced with me until I was out of breath.

After Jud left I was on my own again—except for Joliette. Suzette had vanished. One day, when I had allowed the cats to go ashore, I had seen a big tomcat coming around some garbage cans. He looked with special interest at Suzette. I guessed that Suzette had taken up with this tomcat. Anyway I never saw her again. Joliette was getting larger and I realized she was going to have kittens.

On May 1, I left Pago Pago and sailed south to the Tonga Islands. In Neiafu's harbor all the boats of many different shapes and sizes carried sail. It was like one of those pictures of Boston before steamships were invented. As soon as I had tied up *Dove* at a

(Right) *A kiss for banana pancakes*
(Below) *The Islands have great swimming pools*

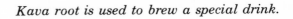

Kava root is used to brew a special drink.

wharf, an old man came towards me and welcomed me to the island. He said he would like me to meet his chief.

Everybody seemed to be happy, and I was surprised to find people so nice to me. Then I remembered that Captain James Cook had named these the Friendly Islands.

When I met the chief, whose name was Kaho, he said to me, "Why don't you stay with us? You will be happy here until the end of the world."

Instead of writing letters, I was sending tapes home. On my tape from the Friendly Islands, I told Mom and Dad, "I'm beginning to discover how different people are—as different as flowers from flowers and trees from trees. Why do we lump people all together?"

The weather was beautiful with sunshine every day and the sea so clear I could see shells on the bottom 14 feet down. I spent a lot of time just cruising about the islands, diving for shells and looking at the fish with fantastic colors. It was here that I started my collection of shells. I boiled the meat from the shells and soon learned which ones made the best meals.

When I was tired of seafood I exchanged some of my ballpoint pens or old clothing for fruit and vegetables. I was always being invited out, even by complete strangers. The island people loved to tell stories. Most could speak good English. I enjoyed just listening to them speaking among themselves in their own language, which was very musical. When they ended their conversations they usually gave a greeting, *"Mal e lelei, mal e foloau."* ("Good day, and thanks for coming.") They had pleasant manners.

At one party I was given another name. Chief Kalaniuvalu called me Kai Vai. He explained that the name means "Eat Water." When I looked surprised the chief said,

The Tongans are always smiling even when they work. They wanted me to stay forever.

"That is the name given to the soldier who sits in the front of a boat to protect the chief from spray. It is a name of honor." I don't know why he gave me this name, but I rather liked it. So after this, when the island people asked me my name, I said Kai Vai. Perhaps that is why they treated me so nicely.

I sailed on to Tongatapu, where I attended a special ceremony called *kilikili*. This ceremony marked the end of six months' mourning for Queen Salote Tupou III, who had ruled Tonga for 47 years. My host invited me to wear a black shirt and black skirt like the other islanders so that I could show my respect for the beloved queen. Around my waist I wore a *ta'ovala* which is a mat of plaited grass. The bigger the *ta'ovala,* the more im-portant the person. The royal chiefs wore mats almost to their ankles.

The Tongans are very religious. Their islands are close to the International Dateline. One Tongan told me proudly, "This is where the earth day begins. So you see we Tongans are the first people in the world to pray each morning."

Two hundred years before I had arrived in the Tonga Islands, Captain Cook had written in his logbook, "Thus we took leave of the Friendly Islands and their inhabitants after a stay of between two and three months, during which time we lived together in cordial friendship."

I had the same feelings as Captain Cook, so I wrote the same words into the logbook of the good ship *Dove.*

I wear a black shirt and skirt to show respect for beloved Queen, who had recently died.

CHAPTER XI

A New Friend

Now I PLANNED to sail for the Fiji Islands, almost due west. I had made friends with other yachtsmen and I set out on the next leg of my voyage with two sleek yachts, *Corsair II* from South Africa and the *Morea* from California. These yachts were bigger and faster than *Dove* and they soon left us far behind.

The wind changed direction and I found myself beating into it. This meant that I had to tack from port to starboard and back, and my progress was slow. When the sea began to get rough, I decided to anchor for two days on the leeward (sheltered) side of the little island of Kambara, where I paddled my small dinghy ashore. I left Joliette in charge of the boat. Joliette had had her kittens but they had been born dead.

On shore some island people asked me if I would take a sick woman to the Suva hospital on the main Fiji island. The family of the sick woman came down and looked over *Dove*. They shook their heads and said that the woman would be in more danger if she sailed in *Dove* than if she stayed at home. So Joliette and I sailed on.

When I arrived in Suva, I had only $23.43 in my pocket, and at first the Fijian people did not want me to come ashore. I guess they thought I would become a bum. But the

Warriors dance to their special music. They are not as fierce as they look.

American consul, who had heard of me, came to my rescue and said he would look after me if I ran out of cash.

It was quite embarrassing to read a headline in the local newspaper which said, "Schoolboy Sails Pacific in a Teacup." Tourists came down and peered at me through the portholes.

The Fijians are a strong, handsome people. Their skins are dark and their frizzy hair stands high on their heads. A little more than one hundred years ago the Fijians were cannibals. The last missionary to be eaten was the Reverend Thomas Baker, who was boiled alive at a feast.

Today, if one Fijian wants to insult another Fijian he says, *"Kana nai vava Baker"* ("Go and eat the boots of Mr. Baker.").

I liked the Fijians. I went to one of their special parties where the women prepared a drink made of kava roots. The drink, called *yaqona,* looks the color of mud and tastes a bit like sawdust. The people drink *yaqona* as Americans drink coffee. While the women were making the drink, the men sang. The drink was handed to me in a coconut shell. I was told that the polite thing to do was to drink it all at one gulp and then to shout, *"Maca!"* ("It is finished.")

After everyone had drunk from the coconut, the men began to dance and to beat their bare chests. The Fijian who sat next to me translated the words of the song. It was all

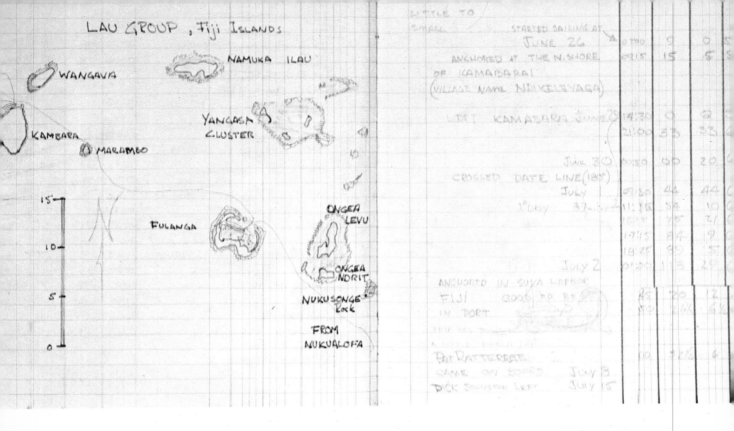

This logbook map shows my route to the Fijis and the day on which I met Patti Ratterree, "The loveliest girl in the world." Patti gave me the courage to complete my lonely voyage around the world. (Below left) Preparing fish for a feast. (Right) Hollowing out a drum.

When the tide went out, it was a chance to remove the barnacles from Dove's *hull.*

about a devil who circled the world and stopped over at places like New York, Cape Town and Sydney. It sounded pretty scary.

Another young American sailor, Dick Johnston, helped me to understand some of the Fijian customs and the language. He also helped me to paint *Dove*. It was good to have a friend of my age so far from home. One evening Dick came down from the yacht club and told me he had heard the name of a California girl whom he had known at school.

The girl was on the other side of the island at Lautoka. Dick decided to take a bus and look for her.

Dick had only just left me when a Fijian waiter came down from the yacht club and asked me if I was missing my cat.

"Joliette?" I asked. "No, I think she's around somewhere."

The waiter shrugged his shoulders and said, "Cat like yours just been run over by truck at clubhouse."

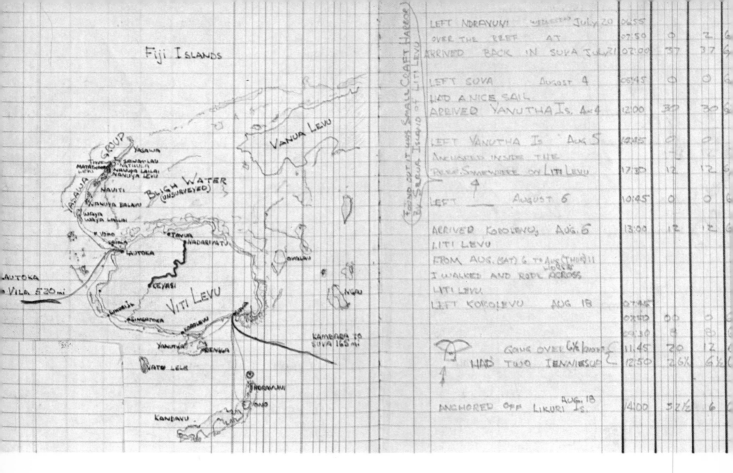

Fiji Islands

My logbook map shows the Yasawa Islands where Patti and I went shell-hunting. There was time to explore which, on Viti Levu, I did on horseback.

I ran up to the clubhouse. In a gutter outside the bar I saw a little crumpled heap of fur. It was Joliette. She was dead. I returned to *Dove* and lay down on my bunk and cried.

Joliette was much more than just a cat. She had been my companion on the high seas. When I was lonely, I had talked to her. Although she could not answer back, just having her around made me feel less lonely. I would have given anything now to have Joliette rub her neck against my ankles or cry for her supper.

That night was the most miserable of my life. I felt more lonely than I'd felt in the middle of the Pacific.

Two days later Dick Johnston awakened me by thumping the cabin roof. He was talking about a girl. I went back with Dick to the clubhouse and there on the lawn I saw Patti Ratterree.

Patti was the prettiest girl I had ever seen. Her teeth were very white and her long blond hair was blowing in the breeze. She was wearing a blue Tahitian dress. Her eyes were blue too, except for a little splash of gold in her left eye. Her eyes sparkled as if they had caught the sunlight.

That evening Patti came back to *Dove* and made Dick and me a very good supper. She

There is always something to do aboard ship, including cooking and dishwashing.

told me a few things about her life. Patti had been born only a few miles away from me in Los Angeles. Like me, Patti had always wanted to find out more about the world. After graduating from high school, she had hitched a ride across the Pacific on different yachts. Her plan was to go to Australia.

Patti had earned money by taking different jobs. She had looked after the children of tourists on one island, and when she had reached the Fiji Islands she had gotten a job as a stewardess on one of the boats which take tourists around the islands. Her job was to know something of the history of the islands and hand out seasick pills when the sea was rough.

But the skipper of her boat was unfair to her and had refused to pay her the money she had earned. She decided to quit her job.

"What are you going to do now?" I asked her as we sat on the deck of *Dove*.

"Find another job, I guess," she said. "Something always turns up."

"What about exploring the Yasawa Islands?" I asked.

"That would be great," she replied.

The Yasawas stretch like an emerald-green bracelet northwest of the main Fijian island.

Patti catches a big fish for our supper.

CHAPTER XII

The Loveliest Playground

TO MOVE OUT of Suva harbor at night was a crazy thing to do, especially as there was no moon. The harbor entrance is about five miles long and very narrow.

On either side I could hear the waves thundering against sharp rocks and coral reefs. There were some navigation lights on the cliffs. I knew that if I lined up the lights I would be able to keep *Dove* in the center of the channel. I could not risk putting up sail, so I used the outboard engine. The swell was so heavy that the engine was often raised right out of the water, when it would roar like a motorcycle.

Patti was seasick. Luckily we made the open sea without hitting any rocks. The dawn was beautiful and Patti cheered up. She came up out of the cabin braiding her long blond hair. She looked pale but she managed to smile. I was glad she had not known how dangerous the night sail had been.

We were just like children in a wonderful playground. The world of cities and traffic, of drugstores and television seemed to be a million miles away. Most days we saw nobody at all.

We would discover a beautiful bay and drop *Dove's* anchor. When the sun had risen

Nothing is more exciting than finding a beautiful bay like the one in the Yasawa Islands.

high enough to light the coral reefs and ledges under the crystal-clear water, we dived for shells.

The shells were like gems. It was like discovering a pirate's treasure chest. After diving for up to 45 seconds, we would explode out of the water, our lungs hurting, and pour our shell treasure into *Dove's* cockpit.

We found violet conches and spotted cowries—shells almost as big as Patti's fist and as smooth as silk. We pounced on the rarer delphinia shells, pagoda periwinkles, murex, and baby moon snails. Other shells were more beautiful than anything a jeweler could make. But some were dangerous.

In my small ship's library I had a book on shells. I was able to identify them as we brought them from the sea floor.

Swimming around under a ledge I saw a small mottled shell not half the length of my thumb. I recognized it from the picture in my shell book. It had a pretty name, cloth-of-gold, and a Latin name, *Conus textile*. But the little shellfish that curled up inside was almost as deadly as a rattlesnake.

Very carefully, with my forefinger and thumb, I lifted up the cloth-of-gold, swam to *Dove* and placed the shell on the top of my drying Levi's. Patti and I waited to see what would happen. A tiny tongue, called a proboscis, came out of the open slit in the shell. The proboscis waved about for a few

Cowries

Cloth-of-Gold

moments, feeling for its enemy—me. Then, with a faint hiss, the proboscis shot out a tiny harpoon into the cloth of my Levi's.

If the harpoon had pierced my finger, the poison it carried could have made me very ill, or even killed me. I had heard how a Fiji Islands tourist had casually picked up a cloth-of-gold which had thrust its harpoon into his palm. The tourist died three hours later.

A few days later I wasn't so lucky. Patti and I swam to some rocks. We were just playing around looking at the rock pools when I saw what seemed to be a little rock moving. That's strange, I said to myself. It must be a shell. I stooped to pick it up.

It wasn't a shell. It was a stonefish, so called because it looks like a stone. But when a stonefish is frightened, it puts out a sharp sting from its dorsal fin.

This one stung my middle finger. It was the sharpest pain I had ever had—much more painful than a wasp sting. Poison from a stonefish can also kill people.

With the help of a friend who knew the South Pacific Islands, I soon learned which shellfish to eat and which were poisonous.

Dove *moored to a buoy in the Fijis. As my logbook records show, the tides and currents could get me into trouble here.*

The nearest doctor was four days' sailing away at Lautoka. Patti had had some first-aid training. She tore the rubber band off her ponytail and made a tourniquet around the base of my finger. Then she told me to suck the wound and to spit out the poison.

One thing we knew was that with the poison in me I must not exercise at all, but try to keep my heartbeats down. Patti rowed me back to *Dove,* and while she was doing this I sucked on the wound and spat out the blood.

Patti rowed to the shore and caught up with a group of island women and girls whom we had seen earlier. She explained in sign language and with drawings on the sand what had happened to me. One of the women could speak a few words of English. She told Patti that I should boil my finger in gasoline!

When Patti returned to the boat with this medical advice, we decided that it would be more dangerous to boil gasoline than to al-

low the poison to do its worst. I even managed to laugh.

Some of the stonefish poison must have got into my bloodstream, because that night I had a high fever. But next morning I felt better. My finger throbbed for three days and I carried the black scar for three months.

At least we had learned that even in this most beautiful playground you have got to know what to play with!

This was the only accident we had, except for a tricky few minutes when I ran *Dove* aground on top of a sharp coral reef. Fortunately *Dove's* fiberglas hull was tough and she suffered no damage.

When we were hungry we dived for clams or fished for mahimahi, the most delicious fish in the Pacific. We experimented with other meals, including squid, which is like a small octopus. Squid does not look too nice, but when it is boiled it makes a great meal.

Everywhere the children were eager to play games. In the South seas the water is always warm,

Sometimes, when we anchored *Dove* in a bay circled by a golden shore, young boys and girls came out of the palm trees to wave to us. Often island children had their arms filled with fruit—papayas, bananas, breadfruit, limes and coconuts. We gave them ball-point pens or old clothing and they gave us the fruit.

It was great to go ashore and to barbecue our fresh-caught fish and then drink the milk of coconuts or a drink made from spring water and fresh limes.

One day I swapped an old pair of pants for a chicken. We named the chicken Henrietta because it reminded me of a pet chicken I had had as a boy and which I had called Henrietta. The chicken looked rather thin, so

we kept it in a banana crate on top of the cabin and Patti fed it rice. One day when we had not caught any fish we decided it was time to broil Henrietta. But Patti had become so fond of the chicken that she didn't want me to wring its neck. But I was hungry. When Patti was in the cabin I went up on deck and took Henrietta out of the crate. So that Patti would not hear Henrietta's last squawks I sang as loudly as I could. Henrietta made a great dinner!

Every day was so wonderful that it was hard even to think of returning from the Yasawa Islands. On the island of Naviti we went ashore and walked to a meadow among the palm trees. Below us, *Dove* was riding at anchor on a sea that was as blue as the sky.

so their playground is the sea or the golden sunny beach.

For a while neither of us spoke because there were no words to describe the beauty and our happiness.

Then Patti suddenly said, "Let's build a house!"

We dashed about pulling down palm fronds and we cut some poles. In half an hour our house was built. It even had a front door which opened on hinges made from leaves. We went inside and knelt together on the grass floor. The sun shone through the little holes between the palm fronds and made a pattern of light on our faces.

Suddenly it didn't seem like a game. Our playhouse seemed like a real house.

Patti and I had fallen in love. If only, I thought, we could live here forever. We could

pretend we were the only people left in the world.

The only sound was the noise of the surf below us on the beach. Patti looked so lovely. I leaned forward to kiss her.

Suddenly our little palm frond house began to shake as if we were having an earthquake. Somebody was beating on the roof.

A gruff voice said, "You in there. You come out. This is my land!"

It was one of the older men of the island. As Patti and I tumbled out into the sunshine, the man waved his stick. We thought this was so funny that Patti and I burst into laughter. So we were not the only people in the world after all! Soon the old man laughed too.

73

GROUP.

YASAWA

SAWA-I-LAU

NACULA

NANUYA

TAVEWA

NANUYA LAILAI
MATACAWA
LEVU
NANUYA LEVU

Somo Somo

YASAWA

NAVITI

NANUYA BALAVU

NALAUWAKI

WAIA

YALOBI

WAIA LAILAI

KOWATA

BLIGH
WATER

VOMO

SAVALAO

10

LAUTOKA

5

KEY

VITI LEVU

GOING TO
SAWA-I-LAU

COMING FROM
SAWA-I-LAU

TO VILA

0

6 KNOTS	07:20	0	0	6346½
	08:20	6	6	6352½
ARRIVED LAUTOKA AUG 20	14:30	37½	28½	6381
LEFT LAUTOKA AUG 23	09:30	0	0	
FOR SAVALA (A.m. WIND FROM			3	
LAUTOKA)				
ARRIVED SAVALA	10:15		3	6,384

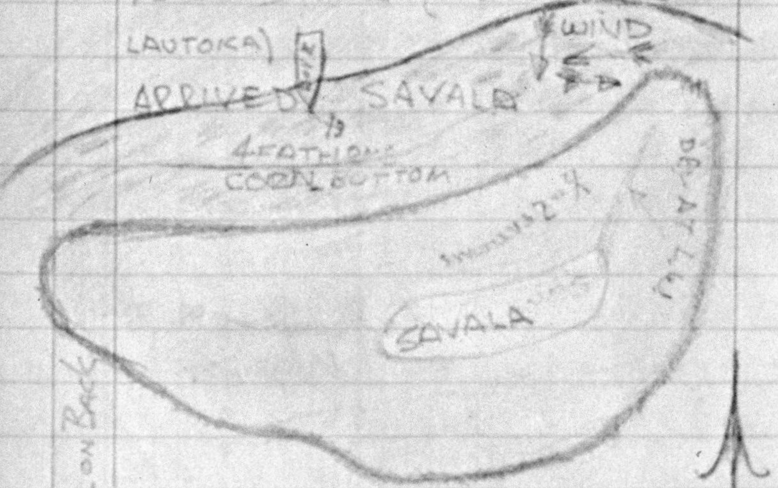

A SAND ISLAND WITH A LITTLE
TBRUSH. (NO GOOD FOR SHELLS)

LAST NIGHT WAS REAL
WINDY AND ROUGH SEAS
WIND WAS FROM THE EAST

LEFT SAVALA AT (AUG. 24)	08:30	0	0	6,384

BOY, THERE ARE SURE
ALOT OF REEFS, AND NO
WIND!

ARRIVED VOMO IS. (AUG 24)	13:40	13	13	6,397

WHITE SAND
VILLAGE

THE VILLAGE IS ON THE NORTH SHORE OF VOMO Is. Fiji

I LEFT VOMO (AUG 25)	09:30	0	0	6397

HAD A VERY NICE SAIL (EAST WINDS)

ARRIVED WAIALAILAI	15:00	14	14	6411

(Written vertically in left margin:)
AUG. 23 (GOT THE BOIL AUG 19) JUST FINISHED A BAD BOIL ON BACK

CHAPTER XIII

Beauty is Skin Deep

PATTI AND I sailed back to Lautoka harbor after the happiest days of my life. There was a letter waiting for me from Dad. He said he had arranged for me to write the story about my voyage for the *National Geographic Magazine*. The money would help me to provision *Dove* with food for the continuation of my voyage.

Dad said he was flying out to the New Hebrides Islands to take some pictures of me. The *National Geographic* wanted many pictures. Dad told me to sail on to the New Hebrides as quickly as possible.

How hard it was to say goodbye to Patti! We did not know if we would ever see each other again. On the night before I sailed, Patti came down to the Lautoka harbor. There was a little bundle of spitting fur in her arms. It was a new kitten.

Patti said, "This is your new mate. His name is Avanga. That's the Tongan word for bewitched."

I took Avanga from her and he scratched my arm. He didn't seem to like his new owner. Then Patti took a gold chain from her neck and hung it around mine.

She said, "It's only a loan, Robin. You can return it to me when we meet again."

Patti had arranged to sail on to New Zealand. She promised to write to me and I promised to write to her. It was almost dark when I paddled the dinghy out to *Dove*. I was glad Patti couldn't see me crying. Perhaps she was crying too.

It was quite a rough sail to the port of Vila in the New Hebrides. This was the same sea that Captain Bligh had sailed after the famous mutiny on the *Bounty*.

It was great meeting Dad again. He told me all the news about Mom, Michael and my friends. But I seemed now so far away from the days when the most important things in my life were ice-cream parlors, bicycles and birthday parties. I was not yet a man, but I wasn't a boy any more. I realized that you can't go backwards in life. Happy memories are great things to have, but more important are the things happening now and what is going to happen in the future.

Dad wanted me to sail on to Honiara in Guadalcanal. He went ahead of me by steamer. I was listening to my radio when I heard a weather report which really worried me. The radio said that there was a hurricane about 120 miles away.

I kept *Dove* close to the coastline. Later I was to find out that the tail of the hurricane had hit my father's steamer. The wind and the sea had been so strong that they had broken the iron railing on the big ship. If little *Dove* had been caught in that hurricane I might not now be writing these words.

A relic of World War II . . . a sad reminder!

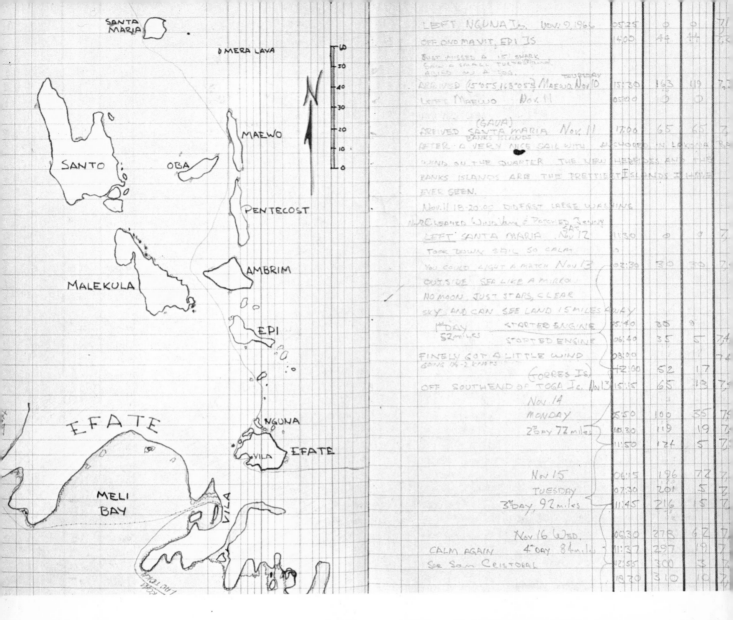

Here are more pages from the logbook of my journey to New Guinea. At Santa Maria the sea was so calm it reflected the stars and I felt like an astronaut in space with stars above and below.

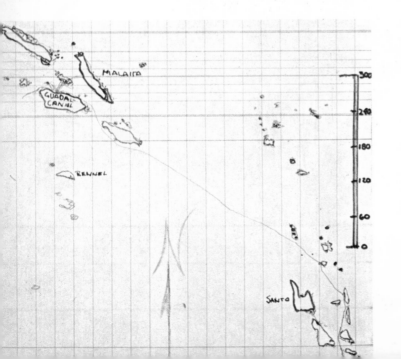

In spite of the hurricane warning, the sea was as calm as a pond. At night even the stars were reflected in the water. It was a really weird feeling sailing through such a calm sea. There were stars above me and below me. I felt like an astronaut traveling in a spaceship.

Avanga didn't enjoy sailing and didn't like me. When I stroked him, he turned around and spat or scratched me. Some cats are just bad sailors—and bad company.

Guadalcanal was one of the places where a great battle was fought in World War II.

Guadalcanal was the scene of many battles fought during the Second World War; but it is so peaceful now it is hard to imagine soldiers fighting there. The log entry shows route to Solomon Islands.

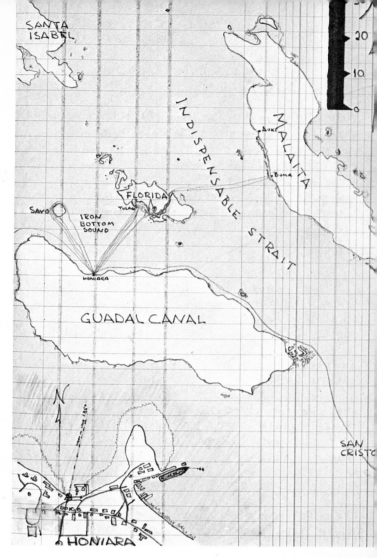

Hundreds of American and Japanese soldiers, sailors and airmen were killed there. Now it was very peaceful. I tried to imagine the warships firing shells and tried to picture airplanes having dogfights overhead. This was difficult for me to imagine especially in the surrounding stillness.

I made friends with an Australian boy who had lived on the island for many years. The boy took me to an old battlefield where he was still finding relics of the great battle. He had found dogtags which had belonged to American soldiers and he sent them to the Pentagon in Washington. I wondered what the relatives of the long-dead soldiers felt when they received these reminders of the Guadalcanal battle.

One of the island men happily showed me a gold watch which he said an American soldier had given to him. The old man whispered, "Me save soldier's life. Soldier give me watch." He did not seem to mind that the watch was not going.

Michael, my brother, was now in Vietnam fighting. I felt close to Michael as I walked about these old battlefields.

Dad arranged with an island chief to have a feast. Dad bought a pig which the islanders roasted in an oven made out of rocks. About a hundred people came to the feast. Most of them were children. Everybody brought along something for the feast—like papayas or *bele,* which is a sort of spinach.

But I did not drink the *kava* made from roots. The custom on this island was for the most beautiful girls to make the *kava* drink. They prepared the roots by chewing them, and then they spat the little chewed-up pieces

Here I am standing on the wreck of a Japanese warship sunk by the Americans. Islanders are still finding dogtags of long-dead soldiers.

I tried on a grass skirt and danced around a bit. (Above) *Women in costume followed in traditional dance.* (Below) *An island native collecting megapod eggs.*

of root into a pot. They said that this old custom made the *kava* especially good. I took their word for this.

Dad shot many pictures of me at the feast and doing other things. Then he flew home again for Christmas with Mom.

At nearby Savo Island I discovered a strange bird called a megapod. This bird has a stubby tail, and it looks a bit like a chicken. It lays eggs in the sand, and each morning the islanders collect the eggs. If an egg is not found, a baby megapod hatches out in about a month. The baby bird is so strong that it can fly as soon as it is hatched. Dad and I watched a hawk swoop down and seize a baby megapod. It is amazing that so many are able to survive humans and hawks.

The islanders gave me a basketful of megapod eggs, but I still don't know what they taste like because I lost them in the surf when my dinghy flipped.

(Opposite) *Islander made his devil mask.*

81

The Solomon children are watching, expecting me to be eaten by sharks.

When visiting Savo Island I usually anchored *Dove* about two hundred yards offshore. The water was almost as warm as a hot bath so I swam ashore. I wondered why the children always came down to the shore to watch me. They seemed excited. Then a boy who spoke some English told me that this was the place where the islanders held funerals. Instead of burying people they drop the bodies into the sea, where the sharks eat them up.

So the children had been expecting me to be eaten up by sharks. After learning about the man-eaters, I never swam there again.

I waited until after the hurricane season before sailing on to my next port, Port Moresby, in New Guinea. On this leg of the voyage I experienced every kind of weather. There was a storm which kept me awake for two days and nights. The angry wind was coming from the west—from the direction in

which I wanted to go. I checked my progress with the sextant and discovered that at one stage *Dove* had actually moved backwards.

Then came a few days of absolute calm. *Dove* sat on the water like a toy boat in a bathtub. It was so hot that the sweat from my forehead trickled down my nose. The drops I blew away splashed onto the bulkhead like raindrops.

Into my tape recorder I reported, "My shirt and pants are so soaked with sweat I might just as well have taken a bath. But what a miserable way to take a bath!"

Unexpected things prevented me from going crazy. One day I heard a little bump against the side of *Dove*. I looked over the rail and there was a huge turtle. I grabbed one of its hind legs and tried to heave the turtle on board. But it gave a kick and swam away. That was sad. I could have had turtle soup for a month.

82

The children were eager to know about the white boy and to help fish or hunt shells.

Sometimes I began talking to myself—just crazy talk. I just had to hear somebody talking—even if it was myself. One day I was sitting in the cockpit talking to myself when the sails, which had been hanging down loosely, suddenly filled with wind.

"That's better," I said aloud to myself, "and about time, too. If I'm lucky I might make Port Moresby before I'm a hundred years old."

Lazily I stretched and looked about to see where the wind was coming from. Wow! Three miles off the port beam a huge black snake-like thing was climbing out of the sea. It was a waterspout.

Sailors call them twisters. You can see miniature twisters sometimes in a park or playground when the wind spins and sucks up the dirt or leaves.

But the twister I was looking at was no baby! It was the ugliest thing I had ever seen. The spout rose out of the water perhaps 2,000 feet. At the top it spread into a black cloud, like an atomic explosion and could be just as deadly.

The wind force on the edge of a twister sometimes reaches 150 miles an hour. If *Dove* got near this one—oh boy, I didn't even want to think about it. And *Dove* was sailing toward it!

I just froze like a deer caught in the headlights of a car. Then I acted fast. I swung the tiller right across. For a few minutes I watched the twister with my heart thumping like a drum. Then the distance between *Dove* and the twister began to increase. You could have heard my sigh beyond the horizon.

I was to face many more dangers later on in my voyage. But every time I remember that twister I shiver.

At last I arrived at Port Moresby. The journey from the Solomons to New Guinea had taken me longer than the sail from San Pedro to Hawaii, which is twice as far. Tired out, I dropped *Dove's* anchor and soon went to sleep.

Taking leave from The Solomons to encounter new dangers.

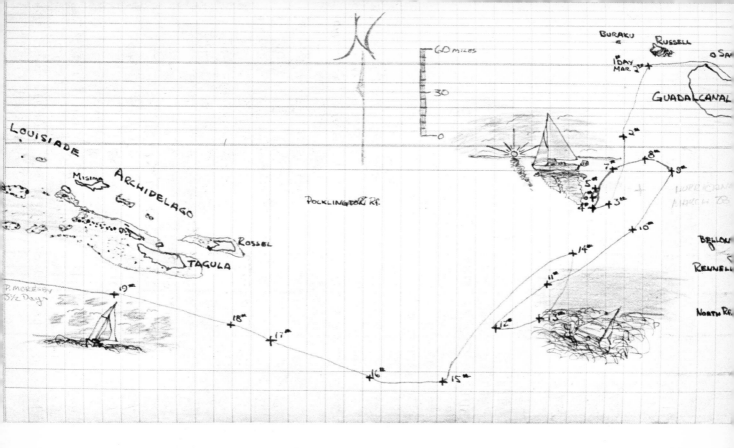

Log map shows how storm blew me backwards—the toughest sailing yet!

Next morning I went to the post office to see if there was any mail for me. I longed for letters from home and I hoped very much there would be a letter from Patti. The post office was closed. I stopped a policeman and asked why. The policeman looked at me as if I was crazy. He said, "It's Good Friday. The post office will be closed until Tuesday."

On the Tuesday I was the first to arrive at the post office. There were letters from Mom and Dad—and from Patti.

Patti wrote that she had arrived safely in New Zealand and had gotten a job working on a farm. She had been able to save enough money to travel to Darwin in northern Australia to see me—that is, if I was going to stop off there.

At sea I had thought so much about Patti. I wanted to see her again more than anything else I could think of. I sent Patti a cable saying I hoped to reach Darwin in about five weeks.

I spent three weeks in New Guinea. Everywhere I went I tried to meet the local people, to understand the way they lived and what they thought. I found that New Guinea is an amazing mixture of the old and the new. Many of the native women are tattooed all over, but in the Parliament many of the native politicians spoke better English than I did. It was a strange combination.

The tattooing is done with a hammer and a thorn. The thorn stabs the skin and little bits of flesh are raised up like bumps.

I watched a young girl being tattooed. She was making the kind of faces I make when I go to the dentist.

My guide told me that in the "good old days" the tattooing did not hurt at all. But that was when it was "a very serious ceremony." The girls were forbidden to laugh. One day a young girl laughed when she was being tattooed. Ever since then, said the guide, the tattooing has been very painful.

I did not allow Avanga to go ashore because he behaved so badly. He chewed up one of my charts. I'm sure he did it just for spite. Avanga and I were not good friends.

CHAPTER XIV

Almost a Collision

THE JOURNEY to Darwin was quite fast going because *Dove* was assisted by a three- to five-knot current for much of the way. I made one stop, at the island of Dalrymple. The island was not inhabited.

At sea I was getting used to the loneliness, though I never enjoyed it. But when I was on land and there was no sign of another human being I began to think that I really was the last human being left on earth. It was much like being Robinson Crusoe without Man Friday.

One dark night *Dove* was sailing along at a good speed and I was reading in the cabin. Suddenly I heard an awful rumbling sound like thunder and than a rush of water. Next moment I was thrown across the floor of the cabin as *Dove* keeled over, almost at right angles. I scrambled to the cockpit and saw an enormous wave, and behind the wave there was what looked like a black wall which towered almost out of sight.

Dove was being run down by a freighter. In the next seconds I expected her fiberglas hull to be crushed like an eggshell. But the bow wave of the freighter threw *Dove* far enough away from the freighter to avoid a

Sitting on the outboard engine one
of the cats watches me clean up Dove.
The cats were great companions
but they never offered to help.

full collision. Yet when Dove's mast swung back it scraped the steel side of the boat.

This was the nearest I had been to disaster. I yelled at the retreating freighter, but no one heard me. The near-collision was partly my fault as my Coleman lamp was not working properly. But there should have been someone on the bridge of the freighter who could have seen my boat and steered the ship away.

Anyway, after this I stayed awake all night every night and slept by day. Then, on a crisp clear morning, I sailed into the harbor at Darwin. The only trouble I had with the harbor people was that they asked me to put down a hundred dollars to make sure that I didn't leave Avanga behind. I guess they saw that Avanga would not have made a good immigrant.

Darwin is a city of new immigrants. After World War II many people from Europe settled here to open up the uranium mines. Because more men than women came to Darwin, they named one of the suburbs Bachelor.

At the cafes I talked to Australians and to the new immigrants including Poles, Czechs, Germans, Hungarians, Greeks and Frenchmen. The new Australians and the Australian-born people got along well together.

The very first thing I did on arriving at Darwin was to go to the post office to send a

On the map: NEW GUINEA · PAPUA · P. MORESBY · ARAFURA SEA · CORAL SEA · VILLE I. · CROKER I. · DARWIN · WESSEL Is. · C. ARNEM · ALMOST RUN DOWN · L. SHIP · CAPE YORK PENINSULA · GROOTE EYLANDT · COOKTOWN · DOVE'S ROUTE FROM PORT MORESBY TO DARWIN · AUSTRALIA · N

On my way to Darwin in Australia I was nearly run down at night by a steamer. (Below) When *the tide went out,* Dove *was left on the mud, but this gave me a chance to check the rigging.*

In Darwin, Northern Australia, Patti and I discovered a natural pool
where we played Tarzan and Jane. But soon we had to part again.

cable home for Mother's Day. Then I sent another cable to Patti in New Zealand asking where she was.

Patti did not get my cable because she was already on her way to Darwin. She traveled by plane, train and bus as far as Alice Springs, in the heart of Australia. There she refused to spend any more of her precious savings on travel tickets, so she started to hitchhike to Darwin.

Now this is really wilderness country which Australians call the "outback." Patti could have walked for days without seeing anyone.

Fortunately she had not walked too far down the dusty road north of Alice Springs when a bus rumbled along. The driver was so surprised to find a pretty blonde girl in the outback that he invited her to travel free to Darwin.

I was inside *Dove's* cabin when I heard my name called from the jetty. I scrambled to the cockpit and squinted across the water. There was Patti and she looked so lovely.

She had changed her jeans for a pretty dress and she had washed the dust of the Australian outback out of her blond hair. It was just great to see her again.

We went off to one of the port cafés, and over a meal of inch-thick steaks we told each other about our adventures.

A photographer from *National Geographic* flew out from Washington to take more pictures of *Dove* and me. I flew with him in a small aircraft to a mission station where there were aborigines, the original inhabitants of Australia.

The aborigines painted pictures of the legends and the history of their people. They painted on tree bark which had been carefully peeled off the trees and dried so that it looked something like cardboard. The aborigines made their paints from the juices of wild berries and from crushed colored stones. Their paintbrushes were made from strands of their own hair!

The pictures were really good. One older artist was painting the aborigine story of the

sun. In their legend, the sun is a woman who carries a flaming torch across the sky every day. At night, the woman puts out her torch and travels underground back to the place in the east where she lights her torch and appears once again.

Of course the aborigines now know what the sun really is. But I laughed with them as they explained their legend to me.

Back in California Dad worried that I was spending too much time on my voyage around the world. He flew out to see me. Dad helped me provision *Dove* and prepare her for the 4,000-mile voyage across the Indian Ocean.

When I sailed out of Darwin, Patti and my Dad were on the wharf, standing side by side. Soon they were tiny dots and then they vanished in the haze.

In the Australian outback I visited, some aborigines showed me their lovely beach and how to peel bark from trees to make "canvases" for painting.

90

The Australian aborigines are among the most primitive people in the world, but they are really good artists. They make their paintbrushes from their hair and use their art to tell the history of their people and their fables. The legend of the sun is a favorite subject found in their paintings. It was interesting to watch them at work. These simple people have discovered the secret of keeping happy.

CHAPTER XV

Man Overboard!

I PLANNED two landfalls in the Indian Ocean —the first at the tiny group of Cocos Islands, and the second at Mauritius.

The first American to sail alone around the world was Joshua Slocum. He had visited the Cocos Islands 70 years before I arrived at the palm-fringed shores. In his sea journal, Slocum had written about his arrival, "I was trembling under the strangest sensations . . . To folks in a parlor on the shore this may seem weak indeed."

But I had exactly the same tingling sensation of excitement when I first sighted the palm trees of one of the Cocos group. There are only about 600 people on the islands, but they are among the happiest in the world. No one could remember when the last serious crime was committed there. When a young couple are married they are given a boat, a house and a sewing machine. Now the Australian Government, who looks after the islands, wants to "civilize" the inhabitants. I just hoped that the natives would not lose their happiness when this happens.

Avanga and I were still not hitting it off. My legs and arms were covered with his scratches. Sometimes Avanga would stand on the cabin roof and jump at me with his claws

In the Indian Ocean, Dove's mast broke so I had to fix up a temporary one. I patched the sail with a towel and shirt. She looked like a hobo but I was proud of her.

wide open. At first I had thought this was his game. But then I realized that Avanga really did want to hurt me. So when I reached the Cocos Islands, I gave him away to one of the Australians at the air-sea rescue station on Direction Island.

The Australians gave me a new battery, because mine was weak and not working too well. I needed it for my lights and to start the outboard engine.

On the day I left I was told that the body of a cat resembling Avanga had been found floating in the surf. I felt bad about this, but I wondered if Avanga had tried to be the cat dictator of the island, and whether the other cats had assassinated him.

In the middle of the night, 18 hours after leaving the Cocos, I heard a weird noise. At first I thought *Dove* must have hit a log or something. But when I reached the deck I discovered that her mast had fallen overboard.

The sails and rigging were in the water too. The twice-broken mast would not be any use to me again, so I cut it loose and pulled the sails out of the water. It was hard work and I took off my safety harness. Then I slipped on the wet deck and fell overboard. If *Dove* had been under sail I would have drowned, but I was able to scramble back again.

"Wow! That was a near thing!" I told the tape. I was still in a very serious situation. I

With her makeshift mast and patched sails, brave little Dove *crossed
2,300 miles of Indian Ocean. This is how she looked when I reached Mauritius.
Many boats have been lost in this long stretch of water. (See route below.)*

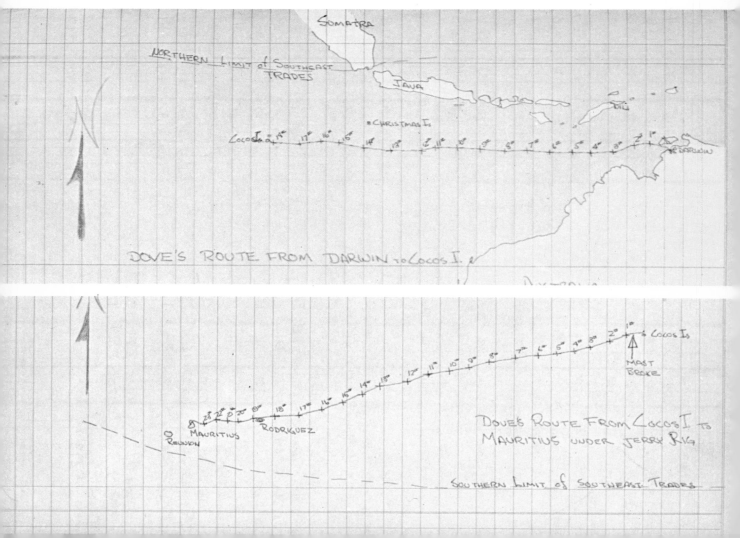

could not turn back to the Cocos Islands because the wind and the current were against me.

For the next hours I just sat in the cabin shivering and not knowing what to do. But the dawn came and I had to do something. I jury-rigged the boom. *Dove* no longer looked like an ocean-going yacht, but more like a cork boat—the kind I used to sail on ponds.

With the shortened mast and small sail, *Dove's* progress would be slow, and I had about 2,300 miles of ocean to cross. I fixed up a second sail with a bed sheet. The wind soon ripped the sheet into small pieces. I was more successful when I made a second sail out of the yellow canvas awning I had used to protect the cockpit from spray.

Dove now moved a little faster and more steadily, but when I looked at my map and realized how far I had to travel, I had a sinking feeling in my tummy. Many boats have been sunk in the Indian Ocean.

But *Dove*, with her home-made yellow sail, traveled more than one hundred miles in the first 24 hours after the accident.

When the yellow sail began to tear, I mended it with a hand towel and a shirt. *Dove* was still far from being a safe boat. Sometimes the swells got so big that half a ton of water was hurled into the cockpit.

I told my tape recorder, "A huge wave just broke over the side. I saw green water through the porthole. Oh boy, are my knees shaking."

Somehow, crippled *Dove* made her way across the Indian Ocean to Mauritius. The strange thing was that the time I took to reach Mauritius was the same as the time I had figured it would take if *Dove* had had a proper mast and mainsail.

At Mauritius there was a cable from Patti. She said, "I will be waiting for you in Durban, South Africa."

I wanted to get going again as quickly as possible. I had cabled the *National Geographic* people in Washington and was surprised and happy when they sent me a new aluminum mast by air freight.

Mauritius is a busy little island where they grow lots of sugar cane. The people are a real mixture of the East and the West. In the streets of the main town, Port Louis, I jostled into Chinese, Indians, Creoles, English and French people. Most of the people seemed to speak French, but fortunately most spoke English too.

When I "stepped" the new mast (the nautical term for putting it in place), I had a small party on *Dove*. So many people climbed aboard that *Dove* began to sink. I had to chase off the party guests and to plug the scuppers before we could continue the party.

There is an old sailors' superstition that when you put up a new mast you must place a coin under it. When I had stepped the mast in Apia in Samoa I had forgotten about this superstition. This time I was careful to place a Mauritian fifty-cent coin under the mast before heaving it into place. *Dove* looked like a real yacht again and I was really proud of her as I sailed out of Port Louis and headed west for Africa.

Ever since I had been a very small boy I had wanted to go to Africa. I had wanted to see the lions and elephants and other animals in their real environment. Just the word Africa made me excited.

A new mast was sent to me from America.

95

CHAPTER XVI

The Great Storm

ON MY seventh day out at sea and near the southern point of Malagasy (it used to be called Madagascar), I saw a black squall on the horizon. I reefed the mainsail and the genoa in case the wind should increase suddenly. I sure did not want to break *Dove's* mast again.

Suddenly the sea began to get rough. I wasn't too worried because *Dove* was a good strong boat. But I had not counted on seas like this. The swells were coming up behind *Dove* and smacking into her stern. The crests of the swells were curling into white combers.

The swells grew bigger and bigger. Now the tops of the swells towered over *Dove*. As she climbed up their sides and slithered into the troughs, she began to groan and shudder. *Dove* seemed to be complaining at having to work so hard.

The wind increased too. I reefed the jib to the size of a handkerchief—just enough sail to keep her on course. There were now two big dangers. The first was that the huge combers smacking into Dove's stern would make her yaw (turn sideways). If *Dove* turned side-on to these huge swells, she would roll over.

The other danger was pitchpoling or corkscrewing. After sliding down a swell, Dove's bow could continue to plow into the water. If this happened the boat would corkscrew under the water or it could somersault.

The sides of the swells were now so steep and high that sometimes it felt as though I was sailing down a waterfall.

There was no chance to sleep. It was dangerous even to leave the tiller. But I had to eat something to keep up my strength and to brew coffee to keep the cold out of my bones.

I was down in the cabin when a huge sea crashed into *Dove*. The boat felt as if it had been kicked by an elephant. I told my tape recorder, "Oh gosh! I really thought *Dove* was going to break up then. Flying objects hit me. Everything loose was hurled about . . . The sea broke into a porthole and green water poured into the cabin."

If another big sea were to hit *Dove* with the porthole wide open, she would have filled with water. I had to get that porthole sealed up again in a hurry. With *Dove* now being thrown about as if a giant was playing ball with her, I did manage to get the plexiglass back into the frame of the porthole.

The swells grew even bigger. Poor *Dove* groaned and moaned at her battering. Everything was soaked. Water sloshed about the cabin even though I kept pumping it out.

Another big sea hit me and cracked the wood of the companionway doors.

Then the thunder came. The noise was fantastic. A brilliant green light from the lightning filled the cabin like a scene out of a horror movie.

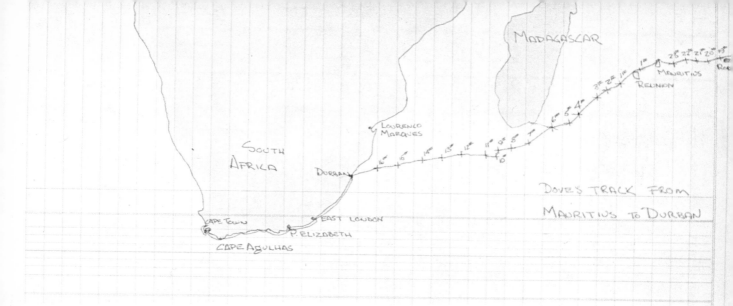

But for two days and nights I did not sleep at all. And still the storm continued. I couldn't keep awake much longer. Every bone and muscle in my body cried out for rest. *Dove* seemed to be saying, "I can't go any further."

For the first time in my voyage I felt I wasn't going to make another port. I thought of Patti. I thought of her waiting for me at Durban. My heart hurt at the thought of her waiting for the blue and white sails to come over the horizon. I loved her so much. What would Patti do if *Dove* never arrived?

Then I remembered a story in the Bible about Jesus calming a sea when a storm threatened to sink a boat.

With my arms hugging *Dove's* tiller, and with the thunder rumbling, and huge seas all around me, I said, "Oh God, whoever you are, please help me. Please help me."

After this I don't remember quite what happened. I must have gone back into the cabin and fallen asleep because I awakened with sunlight streaming through the porthole. I looked out and saw that the sea was just a gentle swell. The wind was down to 15 knots. It was a really lovely day.

I hoisted *Dove's* mainsail and genoa and took a sextant fix on the sun. *Dove* was right on course for Durban in South Africa—right on course for the place where Patti was waiting for me.

Off Madagascar was where the storm struck. I thought I would never see another port. (Below) I sail into Durban, South Africa.

97

CHAPTER XVII

Exploring Africa

PATTI TOLD ME later what had happened to her while *Dove* was in the great storm. She had been staying with friends on a yacht in Durban. The friends had brought her a newspaper which reported, "The yacht *Dove* has been shipwrecked at the Island of Reunion. There was no news of *Dove's* one-man crew."

"It was awful," Patti told me later. She turned to her friend who brought her the newspaper and said, "Robin is still alive. I know it."

Patti checked the story at the newspaper office, but nobody there seemed sure where the report had come from. Every day Patti went out to the breakwater of the Durban yacht basin and waited for the sight of *Dove's* blue and white sails.

Her friends told her, "Patti, you must try to understand that you might never see Robin again. Would you like us to help you to return to America?"

Patti said, "No, I'm waiting for Robin. My heart tells me Robin is all right. He is sailing toward me."

Then on October 21—springtime in South Africa—I saw the high-rise buildings of Durban through the morning mist.

What a wonderful reunion we had! I wanted to marry Patti. I was only 18 years old, but I had traveled halfway around the

Elsa, our motorcycle, parked beside Dove.

world and I felt I had had enough experience of life to know my own mind.

At a little jeweler's shop in Durban I bought a gold ring. I took Patti down to the beach. We sat on the white sand in the sunlight. I put the ring on her finger and said, "Patti, I love you. I just know that I want to spend the rest of my life with you." Later we were married by a South African magistrate.

We were so happy. We bought an old Japanese motorcycle and a pup tent and we set off to explore Africa together.

We had some real adventures on our honeymoon. We called our old motorcycle Elsa, for the lion in *Born Free*. Elsa could not go very fast.

After two days we reached the Umfolosi Game Reserve, which is the home of the famous white rhinoceros. With two of us aboard, Elsa did not like climbing hills. Ahead of us there was a steep hill. Our only chance of reaching the top was to make Elsa go as fast as she could—45 miles an hour.

I yelled to Patti over my shoulder to hold on to me as tightly as she could. Then I turned the hand throttle right over. Elsa kicked up red dust and the one cylinder roared. Just as Elsa reached top speed at the bottom of the valley a rhino came ambling out of the scrub at the side of the dirt road.

A collision seemed certain. Patti told me later she closed her eyes. I still don't know

Patti and I spent our honeymoon in Africa. We heard lions roar and native drums beating and wanted to live there forever.

how we avoided hitting the rhino, the second biggest animal in the world. At the last minute I managed to swerve.

Patti and I were too shaken up even to talk as Elsa climbed the hill. Later, when we pitched our blue pup tent under a tree, we were able to laugh at our narrow escape.

That night, when Patti and I were asleep, we were awakened by something tearing out the shrubbery just outside our tent. I lifted the tent flap and shone my flashlight. All I could see was one big red eye glaring at me about ten yards away.

All I could think of doing was to say, "Shoo!" Nothing happened. The red eye did not even blink.

If the animal was a rhino—and I guessed it was—it must now be deciding whether to trample on us. Perhaps the beast thought our tent was a new kind of animal. Suddenly it rumbled off into the night.

Patti took this picture of me leaning on Elsa in front of a huge anthill.

When the sun went down, we pitched our little tent and cooked dinner over an open fire. After dark, we listened to the cries of animals.

Patti and I did not do much sleeping after this. We listened to jackals making their weird laughing noise. I figured that exploring Africa was more adventurous than being caught in a storm at sea.

How we loved Africa! Elsa chugged and puffed her way down red dirt roads, through little African villages of round houses made of mud and with thatched roofs. The African children came to the roadside and waved to us. Their teeth were as white as pearls.

When we stopped at a village store to buy vegetables, the white Afrikaner storekeepers were so happy to have visitors from far away that they would not let us pay a penny.

We had no calendar and not even a watch between us. When the sun went down, we stopped Elsa and pitched our pup tent. Then we cooked our dinner over an open fire. As night fell, we listened to the beat of African drums and the sounds of animals. When we were near the famous Kruger Park Game Reserve we heard the roar of lions!

We awakened with the sun and often watched herds of impala, the loveliest of the antelopes. If we made the slightest noise, even like breaking a twig, the impala herd would take fright and scamper away—just a flash of brown and white fur against the deep green of the African veld.

We picked up one friendly traveling companion. It was a chameleon about a foot long. We called him Clyde. He was like an animal from another age and looked like a baby alligator. When he walked he sort of lumbered along like an old man. We perched Clyde on Elsa's handlebars as a mascot. One day Elsa skidded on a patch of oil. Patti and I were thrown into a ditch. We picked ourselves up, dusted ourselves down and looked about for Clyde.

Clyde was not hurt, but he seemed offended by the accident. He was walking along the side of the road on the tips of his toes. I put him back on Elsa's handlebars. But now Clyde kept one eye on the road in

We bathed in this waterfall and watched the animals come to drink.

front of us and the other eye rolled upwards to look at my face. Clyde seemed to be saying to me, "Now, Robin, you be more careful because I don't want another accident."

We did not want to turn Elsa back towards the coast. But I knew I had to continue my sea journey. When we arrived at Durban I found that *Dove* had been more damaged than I had suspected by the storm off Malagasy. Water had seeped into the plywood between the deck fiberglas. I had to reseal the deck where it joined the hull. I also removed the cockpit and decked *Dove* over aft. In a heavy sea the cockpit had always filled up with water. *Dove* would be more buoyant now.

The space under the new cockpit deck was like a small additional cabin. Patti called this area "the Cave." Later on I was to find that the Cave was a really nice place to sleep.

Sailing down the South African coast was just about the toughest part of my long voyage. The sea was usually rough and the wind almost always against me, which meant I had to "beat" (sail upwind) most of the time.

Many ships have been wrecked on this coast. One of the most famous wrecks was when the British ship *Birkenhead* was sunk about a hundred years ago. Most of the 638 passengers were soldiers, their wives and children. Only 184 were saved, including all the women and children.

The soldiers on the *Birkenhead* stood at attention on the deck while the women and children got into the lifeboats. Although the soldiers knew that they would soon be drowned, not one soldier attempted to get into the lifeboats. While the ship sank a young drummer boy, probably about 15, beat his drum and gave courage to the other passengers. The drummer boy drowned too.

Back in Durban I removed Dove's *cockpit, covered over the deck and created an extra cabin, called "The Cave."*

103

CHAPTER XVIII

Lost and Found

PATTI RODE ELSA down the coast and we planned to meet up again at the small port of East London. On the map it did not look too far.

Soon after I sailed *Dove* out of Durban the wind changed. On the shore, about five miles away, I could see a big hotel. I was still opposite the hotel after two hours. I was going nowhere. I decided to return to Durban and to wait for a better wind.

Back in Durban it was raining. This big city, which had looked so warm and friendly when I had first arrived there to meet Patti, was now dismal and gray. Patti wasn't there. She had left for East London on Elsa.

I walked along the wet sand to where I had given Patti the wedding ring. It was so lonely and empty now.

Three days later I sailed out of Durban again. Fog came down and it was so thick I could hardly see *Dove's* bow or the top of the mast. I felt even lonelier.

I began to think of all the stories I had been told about ships being lost along this stretch of coast. One steamer, the *Waratah*, which had been sailing for Australia with many passengers, had vanished without trace. They never even found a lifebelt.

All I could hear now were the mournful foghorns of other ships. Since the Suez Canal

Patti's shot of Dove *sailing into a dangerous sea.*

had been closed by the six-day war between Egypt and Israel, the route around South Africa had become one of the busiest shipping lanes in the world.

Lost in the fog, I could not take a sun fix. Luckily, I picked up a radio beacon. The radio beacon sends out signals at regular intervals. By turning the antenna of my radio I could pick up a loud blip noise. Radio beacons make it possible for aircraft to fly safely through fog and thick cloud toward their airport.

I guessed the blip was from East London, so I sailed towards it. The fog suddenly lifted and there was the harbor wall of East London right over my bow. What a relief!

Patti wasn't there. I was really worried about her because she had had to ride Elsa through the Bantu (African) territory called the Transkei. There had been some robberies, and even some murders, in the Transkei. A girl riding a motorcycle alone could easily get into trouble.

At the police station they told me they had had no reports of accidents in the Transkei. I returned to *Dove,* anchored in the yacht basin, and went to sleep. But I had an awful dream. I saw Patti lying in a ditch with the wreck of Elsa beside her. I woke up in a real sweat. It was Sunday morning. There were no people around when I reached the East London sea-front road. The sun slid

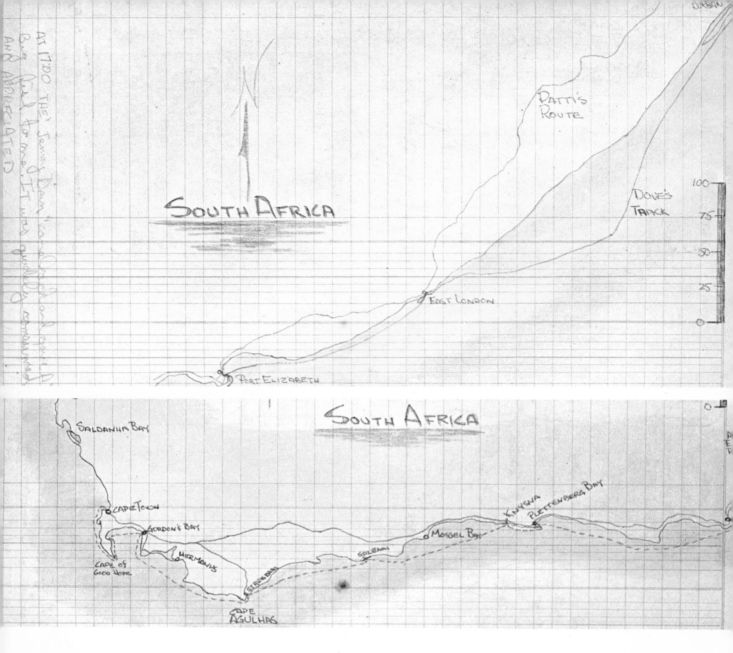

Along the coast of Africa was the hardest sailing of my voyage. Map shows some of the ports of call.

out of the sea and was reflected back from the windows of hotels. Then about half a mile away I saw a tiny figure. I knew it was Patti. We both began running towards each other at the same time.

I hated the idea of sailing out to sea again and of leaving Patti behind. We puttered around on the East London beach and we went to the zoo where we made friends with a lion. Animals seem to know if you like them. This old zoo lion licked our hands and liked to be tickled.

My next port was Port Elizabeth. Patti was waiting for me this time. From now on, whenever I sailed, I knew Patti would be waiting. This thought made sailing easier for me, even when beating into the wind.

Just before sailing around the southern-most point of Africa, at Cape Agulhas, a big storm blew up. I had to dash for the shelter of a small bay. The storm lasted a whole week. *Dove* was again leaking badly at the place where the deck was sealed to the hull, and I was running short of food.

106

I told my tape recorder: "Wouldn't be surprised if my whole stupid boat doesn't simply fall apart any minute . . . My good food is all gone and I'm having to eat from rusty cans left over from the Solomon Islands. Oh man, what a bore this is! Patti must be really worried."

A fishing boat alongside me was taking shelter from the storm. The skipper guessed I was hungry. He brought his boat close to *Dove* and threw me a fish. It was great to have fresh food again after a monotonous week of canned beans.

When I was a week overdue, Patti arranged for an aircraft to search for me. I saw the little red search plane circling over *Dove*. The same afternoon Patti rode down the coast and joined me on *Dove*. It was great to have someone to talk to again, especially someone like Patti!

To prepare *Dove* for the long Atlantic crossing, I pulled her out of the water at Gordon's Bay. There Patti and I painted her

(Above right) *I make friends with a zoo lion at East London, South Africa, and* (below) Dove *is prepared for a long haul across the Atlantic.*

Sailing past the Cape of Good Hope, where the Indian and Atlantic Oceans meet. (Below) Patti helps me with the shopping, stocking up with provisions for the Atlantic voyage.

and, with some help from a fiberglas expert, we sealed up the cracks in *Dove's* deck.

The port captain with whom we had made friends gave me two kittens. We named them Kili and Fili, for the youngest dwarfs in the famous Hobbit books. Fili was blind. No one else wanted a blind kitten. Perhaps that's why Patti and I wanted her.

We spent two weeks in beautiful Cape Town. Sea captains say that Cape Town and Rio de Janeiro are the world's most beautiful harbors. The white houses of Cape Town nestle in the shadow of huge Table Mountain. Most days there is a flat cloud on the top of the mountain and the local people call the cloud "the Tablecloth."

We had arranged for Patti to sail to Europe by steamer, and I was waiting for a good wind from the south before starting the Atlantic voyage.

Patti and I were walking on the beach below Table Mountain when she suddenly squeezed my hand.

"Look at the trees!" she said, pointing to the land side of the beach. I knew at once what she meant.

For two weeks the trees had been bending southwards. Now they were bending to the north. The wind had changed. It was time to sail again.

Two hours later I was sailing away from Cape Town. I left in such a hurry that I had not had time to get all Patti's things off *Dove*. Patti had taken my only comb and my pen. For my voyage across the Atlantic I tried to keep my hair tidy with a wooden Fijian comb. I didn't find any use at all for Patti's bikini!

Patti followed me out of Cape Town harbor in a friend's sailboat. When her boat turned back to shore, I cried. The Atlantic is a huge and, for sailors, a dangerous ocean. I did not know if I would ever see Patti again.

(Above right) *Peter, the friendly seal, called for his breakfast every day at Gordon's Bay, South Africa.* (Below) *Leaving Cape Town for the "downhill" voyage across the Atlantic. I was glad Patti did not see me cry.*

CHAPTER XIX

Across the Atlantic

BEFORE taking *Dove* out of Cape Town, I had installed a two-way radio with a range of about 500 miles. I figured out when Patti's steamer, the *Europa,* would be near enough to me to talk to her.

The first time I tried, it was very frustrating; into the radio microphone I said, "Yacht *Dove* calling *Europa.* Yacht *Dove* calling *Europa."*

No answer. Then I heard Patti saying, "Robin, where are you?"

She could not hear me at all, so I tried speaking to her again that night. It was fantastic hearing Patti's voice in the cabin of *Dove.* This time we could talk. She asked about the kittens, Fili and Kili, and she said she would be waiting for me in Surinam, in South America.

Surinam looked an awful long way away on the map. Soon the *Europa* was out of range of my little radio. I was very lonely.

The wind was good and held from the south. But shipping was always a danger to me. I counted 54 ships in my first week of sailing out of Cape Town. Some steamers came so close that *Dove* rocked in their wash.

I had to stay awake at night to avoid a collision. I kept *Dove's* sail well illuminated and I fixed up a radar reflector on her mast.

Soon the big ships disappeared. I was alone on a gray ocean. Well, I wasn't quite alone. Kili and Fili were with me. Fili, the little

blind kitten, was full of courage. She chased Kili all over the deck. She would crouch and then pounce at Kili, but she usually missed by a cat's length.

Fili learned to find her way around the boat by using her whiskers. At first she would bump into things, but next time around the deck or in the cabin she knew exactly where the danger was. Sometimes I couldn't believe she was blind because she was so clever at avoiding obstacles. Fili knew the sea was her enemy.

Another thing I noticed was that blind Fili was much the more independent of the two. Kili liked to jump on my lap and be stroked. But blind Fili did not want to be petted.

I remembered a blind person who did not like to be fussed over either. Blind people want to prove to themselves that they can get along on their own. They are proud of being able to live almost normal lives without being able to see.

As *Dove* approached the equator, a flying fish jumped aboard. Blind Fili had much better hearing than Kili. She was always first to hear the plop of a flying fish arriving. She was out of the cabin with a flash of fur to pounce on the fish before her sighted brother had even stretched and yawned.

Nearing the equator again, the best part of the day was a seawater bath.

110

One morning when *Dove* was sailing along at a good speed, I saw something orange floating in the water just over the bow. I moved the tiller over and scooped up a glass Japanese fishing float. Two small crabs were clinging to the float. They would die if I flung them back into the water. The sea was very deep here, and if the crabs sank to the ocean floor the pressure of the sea above them would have crushed their bodies.

I made the crabs a little raft from the styrofoam lid to my ice chest. So that the crabs wouldn't be hungry, I picked two barnacles off the hull and put these on the raft. Perhaps the raft would be washed ashore.

When it floated away in *Dove's* wake, the little crab raft was the smallest boat on the Atlantic. Anyway, it just made me feel good that the two little living creatures would have a chance of survival.

It was important to find something to do. In South Africa an old lady had taught me how to crochet, and I made myself a woolen cap with flaps to go over my ears. It sounds silly for a boy to crochet, but I found it rather fun. I read a lot too. I especially enjoyed the Hobbit books and a book called *The Robe* about a Roman soldier who had been given the robe which Jesus wore when He was crucified.

On July 22 I told my tape recorder: "Started my voyage around the world three years ago today . . . It seems like I've been sailing all my life." I celebrated this "birth-

There were always new creatures to see, including this land crab scuttling across the landscape of Ascension Island, and the turtle, which paddled across to Dove, *as if to say, "good morning."*

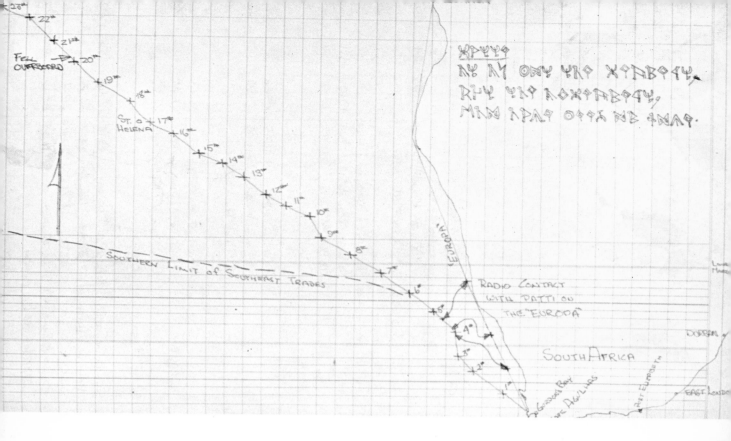

Logbook records my journey across the South Atlantic.

day" with some pickled fish which Patti had bought me in Cape Town. Patti and I just loved pickled fish. But when I started eating them, I missed Patti so much that I began to cry like a baby. I threw the pickled fish overboard.

Twenty-three days after leaving Cape Town I arrived at Ascension Island, which has become one of the important deep-space tracking stations. As it was quite late in the evening, I decided not to go ashore but to fish for my supper. I hooked a six-pound bonito which I hung over the side of the boat, and then I thought it would be good to go for a swim in the beautifully clear water.

Suddenly a huge shark swam by and snapped my bonito clean in half. If I had been swimming, it might have been my leg that the shark would have eaten.

Next day I went ashore in *Dove's* dinghy. The Air Force people who operate the tracking station gave me a good dinner. The senior officer at the base scowled at my bare feet. Another Air Force man took me around the

island, and I discovered a heap of old grog bottles—the remains of a pirates' dump of 200 years ago.

With *Dove* stocked up with fresh milk and vegetables, I set sail again, now taking a course west-north-west across the South Atlantic to Surinam in South America.

Most days I did the same thing. I would usually go to sleep at about nine or ten at night and awaken when the sun was about fifteen degrees above the horizon. After taking a fix on the sun with my sextant, I would look at the taffrail log-spinner and work out how far I had traveled. The wind was mostly from the east and fairly steady. As *Dove* sailed further across the Atlantic the speed of the east-west current increased, so the actual distance I traveled each day over the bottom increased too. In fact, on one day I set a new record for *Dove*—185 miles in 24 hours.

Mostly I was able to sail with two jibs, wing-and-wing. I guess that anyone looking down on *Dove* from an airplane would have thought he was looking at a big butterfly.

On Ascension Island's volcanic landscape, I felt like a moon explorer. (Below) *My route to South America.*

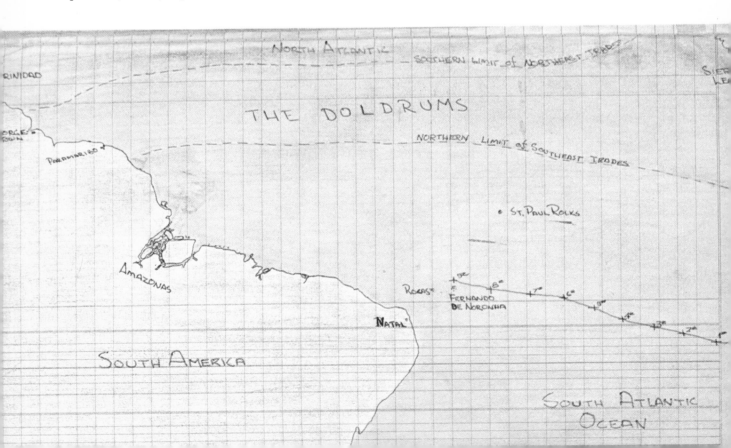

Robin and Kili, companions at sea.

After entering my position in *Dove's* logbook, I made myself breakfast, perhaps bread, canned fruit and coffee. Then I took a bath by filling up my canvas bucket with sea water and pouring the water over my head. The bath was always refreshing and I really looked forward to it.

In the afternoon I read for a while and then in the evening, over another meal, I sat in the cockpit and thought about Patti and my future. Sometimes I listened to the radio and picked up foreign stations. I wished I could understand what they were saying. I listened to the news from the BBC (the British Broadcasting Corporation) and the Voice of America.

Forty-three days after leaving Cape Town I sailed up the Surinam River and anchored *Dove* off the bustling town of Paramaribo.

What a mixture of people—Indians, bush Negroes, blacks, whites, Chinese, and they all seemed to get along fine together. They laughed at me because I was always barefooted.

Surinam, a Dutch protectorate, was one of the first countries to free its slaves. Most of the freed slaves decided not to go back to Africa. Some descendants of the slaves are now quite wealthy farmers. The flag of Surinam has five colors for the five different skin colors of the people.

The first thing I did when I arrived was to look for Patti. She was not there. Patti had visited several countries in Europe. She loved Spain, France, Switzerland and England. But, like me, she had been lonely.

In one letter she said, "All the time I just wanted to show you things, Robin. I loved the old streets and the feeling of history . . . I wanted to talk to you about these wonderful places. But you were not there beside me . . . One day, Robin, you and I will come back and see these places together. We will buy another Elsa and explore Europe as we explored Africa. One day . . ." Patti took a steamer to Trinidad. I sent a cable to tell her I had arrived. I said, "Take a supersonic plane or a satellite for Paramaribo."

115

CHAPTER XX

Indian Country

BEFORE PATTI ARRIVED I had the chance to explore real Indian country in the interior of Surinam. Children at an Indian village took me fishing for piranhas.

Piranhas must be the most dangerous fish in the world. They attack in large numbers and can strip the flesh off a horse in about ten minutes. The Indian children told me that if I fell into the lake the piranhas would gobble me up in about two minutes. I sure was careful.

The Indians let me stay in one of their thatched-roofed homes. Some small boys took me shooting, not with guns but with bows and arrows. They were so good that they could shoot down a small bird. I was so bad with a bow and arrow that at first I couldn't hit a can at ten yards. But I improved.

Then the children took me swimming.

"Not me," I said, thinking about the piranhas. They laughed and explained through an interpreter who was a missionary that piranhas don't live in fast-running water. I had a great time splashing around with these happy Indian children, but I had a nasty feeling that a piranha would wander out of the lake and take a hunk out of my leg.

At Surinam the Indian children took me swimming, and I showed them how to fly—almost!

On Sunday the Indian children took me to church. As they were very poor they did not have special clothes but wore their usual ones—just tiny aprons fore and aft.

One of the missionaries gave me a beautiful green parrot. The bird talked only Indian language, so I did not know whether it was being rude or polite when it sat on my shoulder and jabbered away.

Then I received a message that Patti was coming. After arriving in Paramaribo, Patti boarded a small four-seater aircraft for the mission station. At the jungle landing strip I watched the plane touch down. Patti jumped out and ran towards me. I ran towards Patti. The parrot was scared by all the commotion and flew away. But it was great to hug Patti for the first time in exactly two months.

Back at Paramaribo, Patti and I set up house in *Dove*. It was not easy living in *Dove* because the boat was so small that we bumped our heads on the cabin roof every time we stood up straight.

Dove had been a good boat. She had sailed me through storms and doldrums, across oceans and to so many exciting places. But *Dove* was beginning to crack up. Water had again seeped into the wood of her deck, and I feared that she might break up in another big storm. I did not want to sail her out into the ocean again.

Indian children love games. I showed them a conjuring trick with disappearing sticks; they showed me how to catch piranhas, vicious flesh-eating fish.

And I was beginning to crack up too. Those long days and longer lonely nights at sea had really got to me.

The *National Geographic* people, who had been paying me for telling my story, said that they would help me buy a new and bigger boat to complete the voyage around the world. But first I would have to sail north to the West Indies.

At first I refused. "Why should I sail any more?" I demanded.

Patti was silent for a moment, and then she said quietly, "Robin, I believe you are meant to finish what you set out to do."

"Do you want me to prove that the world is round?" I asked crossly.

"No," said Patti quietly. "I think there is a reason for this trip, even though we don't understand the reason now."

We got out the atlas again. I had sailed 22,000 miles and about three quarters of the

At Surinam I had to keep Kili away from my parrot. It was great to have Patti around to wash my shirts, cook my dinner, and to bargain at the local food market.

way around the world. Perhaps, I finally thought to myself, the last quarter won't be all that long.

So Patti sailed out of Surinam in a steamer for Barbados, in the West Indies. I sailed *Dove* on the next leg of my journey.

At Barbados, Patti was waiting for me. We found a little apartment overlooking a white sandy beach and a sheltered cove where I anchored *Dove*. The scene was more beautiful than any picture.

Mom flew out from California to join us. She had never met Patti, but they went shopping together and soon got along really well.

It was great to sleep in a real bed again—a bed that didn't move about with every wave and change of wind. I enjoyed hot showers, too. Then Patti and I rented a motorcycle and we toured the lovely island. Mostly we just loved being by ourselves. Our favorite picnic spot was under some trees on a grassy

hill. I liked to lie on my back on the grass and just look at the clouds scudding along and feel the solid earth under me.

Soon I felt a whole lot better. Patti and I flew to Fort Lauderdale to look for a new boat. Eventually I found just what I was looking for. Patti launched the new *Dove* with a bottle of California champagne. But whenever we spoke of the two boats, we always talked of big *Dove* and little *Dove*.

Saying goodbye to little *Dove* was really hard. Patti and I painted her and polished the brightwork, then tied on a big red "For Sale" sign to her poop deck. I just hoped little *Dove* would like her new owner.

Patti and I sailed big *Dove* around little *Dove* in a last salute. The little *Dove* looked so pretty. My eyes were misty as we sailed away in the new boat.

Big *Dove* was faster and sturdier than little *Dove*. Patti and I spent many months just exploring the beautiful islands in the Carib-

Patti and I spent many months exploring the islands in the Caribbean.

120

Little Dove *and big* Dove *side-by-side in the Virgin Islands. It was hard to say goodby to little* Dove *which had carried me two-thirds of the way around the world.* (Below) *Exploring a cave.*

bean Sea. Then Patti boarded a steamer for the Panama Canal and I sailed westwards again.

Fili and Kili were still my companions. Of course, now they had grown into cats. They no longer spent all day chasing each other's tails. They liked to lie on the deck and soak up the sun.

After sailing 1,099 miles towards the Panama Canal, I anchored *Dove* off Porvenir in the San Blas Islands, where I had planned to meet up with Patti again. I rowed ashore in the dinghy and went straight to the only hotel. As I walked up the steps of the hotel, Patti came flying out.

The first thing she told me was that we were going to have a baby.

A few days later we reached the Panama Canal. Patti had picked up quite a lot of Spanish. She had learned some Spanish at school, and now it was coming in really useful. She was able to bargain for food at the market. As we had made a lot of new friends we decided to give a party for them.

We decided on a Hawaiian *luau,* which is a feast of roast pig. First we had to find the pig. We went to a small farmhouse and knocked on the door. A huge man came out, dressed in full armor like a Conquistador. The man had made the armor out of old tin cans, but his sword was real and he seemed quite angry. For a moment I thought I was back in the days when Spain ruled Central America. Anyway, I did not wait long enough to see if the tin-can Conquistador would draw his sword, and I did not know why he was angry. We fled.

At another farmhouse I found a game of cockfighting in progress. Razor blades were

*Preparing a feast of roasted pig
for our friends at Panama.*

tied to the feet of the fighting cocks. Then two cocks were put into a small ring and the birds tore at each other until one cock was badly wounded or killed. The people watching the fight placed bets on their favorite bird. It is a cruel sport and it made me sick.

Eventually we did find a pig and roasted it on the beach. Our 30 new friends arrived for the feast, and we had a great time.

At one of the places we visited before going through the Panama Canal we found a number of white-skinned Indians. They were the descendants of the albino Indians first discovered by the Spanish explorers 400 years ago. The Spaniards had been very excited by their discovery. When the explorers returned to Spain they reported that they had found a colony of Europeans who spoke a rather strange language.

Taking a boat through the Panama Canal is quite difficult because the water in the locks really swirls about. I was quite confident because I knew how *Dove* would behave in any conditions. But the Panama Canal Company law is that all boats must be handed over to one of their pilots. Four linesmen came aboard *Dove* to pull her through the locks. It was not easy to hand over the control of my boat to a stranger. We sailed through the first lock with a tug between *Dove* and the wall of the lock. I was worried that *Dove* was going to be crushed. For most of the way through the Panama Canal, *Dove* was pulled by linesmen on both shores.

Eventually we arrived with hardly a scratch at Balboa, on the Pacific side of the Canal. It was quite exciting being back on the Pacific again after four and a half years.

I was still a long way from home at Long Beach, California, but there was one more place I wanted to visit before "completing the circle of the world." I had read so much about the Galápagos Islands and the strange animals there. So instead of turning *Dove* north to California, I sailed south to the Galápagos off the coast of Ecuador. Patti planned to fly to the Galápagos and join me in two weeks or so.

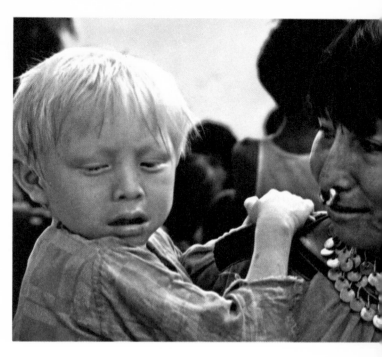

(Above left) *The San Blas Indians are very artistic, as can be seen from their clothes.*
(Above right) *Albino Indians were first discovered by Spanish 400 years ago.*
(Below) Dove *looks small as she goes through the Panama Canal.*

CHAPTER XXI

The Enchanted Islands

IT TOOK ME only eight days to reach Wreck Harbor on the Galápagos Island of San Cristóbal. But it was a very dark moonless night when I arrived. *Big Dove* was equipped with a fathometer, an instrument which can measure the depth of the water under the hull by sending down radio bleeps to the sea floor. A dial in *Dove's* cabin recorded how long it took for the bleep to bounce back from the ocean floor. Even though I had charts of the harbor, it would have been dangerous to sail into a strange harbor in darkness without a fathometer, or by frequently measuring the depth of the water with a leadline.

Until the invention of the fathometer, a leadline was used by sailors to find out the depth of the water over which they were sailing. But taking depth with a leadline is a clumsy business, and it is really hard to haul up several fathoms of rope every few minutes. If I had not had a fathometer I would have stayed outside the harbor until daylight. It was quite spooky sailing through the inky night and just trusting the readings of the fathometer.

Fili was going to have kittens but she had picked up an infection and was really sick, so the first thing I did next morning was to find a doctor, who gave Fili a penicillin injection.

Excited at seeing my first view of the Galápagos.

She soon recovered and gave birth to two kittens which I named Pooh and Piglet.

After a bit of a delay, Patti flew into the Galápagos and we began our adventure of exploring these exciting islands, where most of the animals have no fear of human beings.

The sea lions were just like kids on a playground, the way they wanted to have games with us. One sea lion had a great underwater tug-o'-war with Patti. It used a stick instead of a rope. The sea lion won. The sea lions are terrific surfers and know instinctively just how to catch a wave.

Although the Galápagos Islands are on the equator, the currents here are very cold. When Patti and I swam about for half an hour we were really shivering. Soon we learned to follow the practice of the marine iguanas, known as "the gentle dragons." When they get cold, they climb up onto the rocks and just soak up the sun. The rocks reach a temperature of 120 degrees in the midday sun, and unless you are wet you can easily get blistered. So after swimming, Patti and I just lay around with the gentle dragons all around us. We soon thawed out.

Patti had become a pretty useful sailor, and it was great to have a mate when we sailed around the Galápagos Islands. Patti was also a good cook, and she could use a spear gun to catch our supper from the sea.

We cooked lobsters or fish and then ate from a table which I had slung from the boom. Sometimes there was so little wind that we could eat by candlelight. We'd pretend we were in a posh restaurant and that our orchestra was the noise of the sea splashing up the beach and hitting the rocks.

Sometimes we felt as if we were the only people left on the earth, because for days we never saw another human being. Of course we had visitors—the friendly porpoises. They would swim around *Dove* and then turn on their sides to look at us. They squeaked and laughed among themselves and we always welcomed them.

Ashore we found caves which were used by pirates long ago. When the Spanish ships, loaded with gold, sailed down the west coast of America, the pirates used the Galápagos Islands as a hideout from where they attacked the galleons. When we went into the caves we almost expected to find chests full of treasure. At one place, called Buccaneer

While Patti has a tug-of-war with a sea lion, another gives me a long stare, turns and swims away.

The Galápagos are called the enchanted isles, and even have dragons.
This one is a marine iguana. (Below) *An immature booby rests on* Dove.

Cove, we half-closed our eyes and imagined we could see men with wooden legs and patches over their eyes walking among the lava rocks.

The birds of the Galápagos are as fascinating as the animals. At Hood Island, the southernmost of the group, the mockingbirds were so tame that they flew to our shoulders. These birds are always looking for fresh water. If we held out a teaspoonful of fresh water they would squat on our wrists and suck every drop.

We spent hours watching the marine iguanas, which can change their color from red to green—mostly at the mating season. A baby seal wriggled up to Patti and nibbled at her fingers. The small booby birds did not seem to be afraid to be lifted up. Some of the tortoises were so big we could ride on them. We had a race on two huge tortoises. Patti won.

When we grew tired of eating lobster—and it is the best-tasting lobster in the world—I went hunting for wild goat. One of the islanders loaned me a gun which must have belonged to his great-great-grandfather or a pirate. It looked right out of a museum, but it shot fairly straight. I managed to shoot two goats.

The goats were imported to the Galápagos by fishermen, but they have overbred, and if their population were not kept down they would eat too much of the vegetation. Patti and I sure enjoyed the change in diet.

One morning I threw some fish scraps over the side of *Dove* and some pelicans—which are sort of unpaid garbage collectors—flew across to clean them up. One pelican had a huge tear in its pouch. All the fish scraps it scooped up fell out of the wound.

We figured it would soon die of starvation, so I dived into the sea and grabbed the clumsy bird and brought him back to the deck of *Dove*. Patti broke open the first-aid equipment and I stitched up the wound with nylon. The pelican's beak had been broken, and I mended the beak with stainless steel. The operation took about two hours.

Hunting wild goats gave us a welcome change of diet. (Below) *Painting "Dove" on the side of a rock.*

We saw a pelican with a gash in its pouch. I wired it together with stainless steel.

The next day the pelican returned to *Dove,* and this time it ate twice as much as any other pelican. I guess he was pretty hungry.

Everything on the Galápagos Islands was so beautiful and peaceful that we just wanted to stay there forever. The strange animals had not always been left in peace. Long ago the whaling ships and the merchantmen stopped at the Galápagos to take on fresh provisions and water. While there, the sailors killed thousands of animals just for fun, and they loaded down their ships with huge tortoises.

Half a million tortoises were taken away by the sailors. Now there are only about 10,000 left. Today the government of Ecuador has stopped people killing and capturing the animals (except for wild goats) and the birds. Now people from all over the world visit what the Spaniards called Las Islas Encantadas—The Enchanted Islands.

But it was time for us to leave because Patti would soon be having her baby. Sadly we turned *Dove* about and sailed back to James Bay, on the Galápagos' James Island, where a steamer would be putting into port.

CHAPTER XXII

Homeward Bound

EVEN BEFORE starting the last leg of my voyage, I sensed it was going to be the hardest. I had read stories of sailors who had made long voyages and who, on their last journeys, had been wrecked or who had just vanished without a trace.

The thought that I would never return home—that there would be some disaster, like *Dove* springing a leak—kept on cropping up in my mind. Fear is so often a liar. It is so easy to imagine the things that can go wrong or that they will be much worse than they are. Then we are scared to do what we know is the right thing.

While I was battling storms I had never been really frightened—except for that storm off Madagascar. Perhaps I was too busy to be frightened. But now I was unreasonably worried. From the moment when I watched Patti's steamer sail away at night from the Galápagos Islands, I kept on thinking that I would never see her again. And to see Patti again was what I longed for more than anything else in the world.

The lights of Patti's steamer twinkled and then disappeared. I returned to *Dove* and pulled up anchor. Just before dawn I saw a strange light in the northeast sky. It was a comet, with its tail streaming away from its point.

"That's a good sign," I told Fili and Kili, Pooh and Piglet. Then I told the tape record-er, "There is something missing, though. There is a great big feeling of emptiness inside this boat. I'm 21 years old but I cannot fight back the tears . . . Where is Patti?"

Some yachtsmen had taken up to four months to sail from the Galápagos to California. I had enough food and fresh water aboard *Dove* for 90 days. The freezer was filled with wild goat meat. The cats would not be hungry either. There was plenty of powdered milk, canned chicken and sardines.

My plan was to sail close to the equator, due west for about four hundred miles, and then due north past the tiny islands of Clipperton and Clarion. Long Beach itself was 2,600 miles away. I did not want to make any landfalls before reaching Long Beach.

What I dreaded most was the doldrums. Once again *Dove* had to cross this belt of windless sea. But the voyage started well. Usually there is little wind near the Galápagos. Surprisingly, on the night I set out, quite a strong wind came up and from the right direction. *Dove* scudded along and this cheered me up. I told the tape recorder, "Someone is sure looking after me!"

In my first five days *Dove* made 300 miles. Then I hit those awful doldrums.

On the last leg of my journey I had a strange fear that a steamer might run me down, so I kept a close watch on the horizon.

One thing about sitting in a boat which is hardly moving is that you have plenty of time to think. At night I lay on my back and looked at the stars, as bright as diamonds.

I knew that some stars were so far away that if I traveled at a million miles an hour I would take millions of years to reach them. I thought how many of the stars are thousands of times bigger than the sun. The stars made me feel very small.

Some of the stars were almost friends now. I had learned to navigate by them. It was always exciting to take a fix on a star and to know my exact position.

And my old sea friends, the porpoises, came to visit me. They seemed to know I was lonely. I always felt much better after a visit from the happy creatures.

The cats helped too. Pooh and Piglet were growing up quickly. One morning I awakened and called Fili and Kili for breakfast, but blind Fili did not come. I thought she must be still sleeping in the cabin or else feeding the kittens.

But Fili wasn't in the cabin. Pooh and Piglet were mewing for breakfast. I searched everywhere for Fili, but she was gone. That brave blind cat which had accompanied me for so long must have fallen overboard in the night. There was a quick sharp pain in my heart as I thought of her struggling for her life in the sea.

After this tragedy, Kili looked after Pooh and Piglet. Of course, he had no milk for the kittens, but Pooh and Piglet soon learned to eat fish and drink powdered milk.

At night Kili allowed Pooh and Piglet to snuggle up to him. Sometimes they would snuggle up to me. We kept each other warm.

One thing I found out about sailing alone is that it is important to have something to do. If I hadn't got anything to do, the days just dragged. So I looked around for work. The cabin needed some cleaning up or a piece of gear needed mending or I made some special food like fudge or salt-water bread. My fudge was as sticky as glue and the salt-water bread was so heavy that I was

When Kili was not looking after Pooh and Piglet, he was always ready to play.

Making radio contact with fishing boat, Olympia;
skipper relayed message to Patti.

careful not to fall overboard. I don't know why the bread turned out so badly because Patti was good at making it.

This is Patti's recipe:

1½ cups of sea water
1 tablespoon of sugar
1 tablespoon of dry yeast
4 cups of flour

Melt the yeast and sugar in the salt water, add the flour and stir well. It is not necessary to knead the dough. Grease a heavy pan with butter. Put the dough in the pan and set it aside in a warm place for two hours—say in a patch of sunlight. The warmth makes the yeast rise. Then cook the dough over a low flame for half an hour on each side. It is not the best bread in the world but is a good substitute for the real thing.

I ate more on this leg of the voyage than at any other time since I had set out from Long Beach. The weird thing was that my weight remained exactly the same. I had grown a couple of inches since I was 16, but I was still exactly 150 pounds.

On the morning of my 25th day at sea I made radio contact with a fishing boat, the *Olympia,* about 200 miles away, off the coast of Baja California. I asked *Olympia's* skipper to send a message to Patti in Long Beach, where she was staying with her father.

That night *Olympia* radioed back to me that they had given my message and my position to Patti's father. I told my tape recorder, "Great! Now at last Patti will know where I am. I feel close to her again."

I figured *Dove* was 675 miles from Long Beach, but the wind was coming from the north. That night I felt very depressed and worried that *Dove* would hit a rock or a whale, or perhaps collide with another boat while I was asleep.

A news bulletin on my radio reported that the Apollo 13 astronauts were returning from their space journey. In one week the astronauts had traveled about a hundred times as far as I had traveled in five years! Their homecoming to their splashdown in the Pacific was much more dangerous than mine. So I stopped being sorry for myself and sailed on.

133

CHAPTER XXIII

The World is Round

THESE LAST FEW days at sea were as long as the week before Christmas. Even Kili began to go crazy. Kili had no mice to chase, not even a leaf to play with. He would just stare at the wall of the cabin and suddenly the hair on his back would rise as if he was terrified. Kili hated my fishing knife, which I wore in a leather sheath on my belt. I felt little taps and looked down, and there was Kili with a frightened look just padding away at the sheath. Sometimes Kili just sat on my bunk and cried. I felt like crying too, especially when *Dove* beat into strong headwinds and made no headway.

But Pooh and Piglet were happy. They had grown big enough to scramble out of the cabin to the deck, and they were good about using the litter box.

The weather suddenly became cold and the seas rougher. With the wind coming straight from the direction into which I wanted to sail, all I could do was to tack.

One day *Dove's* taffrail log-spinner recorded that I had traveled 120 miles, but when I managed to get a sun fix I discovered that I had actually traveled only 25 miles towards Long Beach.

I was asleep at night when I was awakened by a change in the wave pattern on the hull. I jumped to the deck and found that the

First sight of home earned a big grin.

wind had swung around the compass to the east. That was better. *Dove* "took a bone in her teeth," as sailors say, and scudded along in great style.

On the night of April 28, my 38th day at sea since leaving the Galápagos, I sniffed a vaguely familiar smell—rather like the smell of wet concrete. This puzzled me at first. Then I recognized what the smell was. It was smog. Even that was welcome.

No one has ever been happier to smell the Los Angeles smog than I was. I stood on the cabin roof and saw a glow in the sky from a city of millions of people.

I got out my tape recorder and sat on the cabin roof. Into the microphone I said, "Just can't believe it! My stomach is all knotted up. This is what I have dreamed about for so long. Home tomorrow!"

With a blanket wrapped around me to keep out the cold, I told the tape recorder, "Those must be the lights of Santa Catalina Island. Good old Catalina! And just look at that moon. It's like the moon the cow jumped over! . . . California, you sure stink! . . . Thirty-eight days without seeing anybody." Can you imagine my excitement?

But for most of my last long night at sea I just thought about all the things that had happened to me over the past five years. I thought about all the people who had been so kind to me.

Sailing alone, it is important to have something to do, like mending the gear.

Kindness, honesty and laughter, and just the simple thing like people looking after each other, have nothing to do with money or how important you are. I thought about this. I thought about the many times I had just left *Dove* with the cabin door open alongside places where the poorest people lived in grass huts. But nothing was ever stolen.

People who live on the islands and in Africa and other faraway places seem to be happier than many people who live in big homes and who drive new automobiles.

Perhaps the most important lesson I had learned was how little a person needs—not how much.

At ten o'clock that night I managed to talk to Patti on my radio telephone. She

136

promised to be at the entrance to Long Beach harbor at dawn. She and her father were coming out to the breakwater in a powered cruiser.

Now I really felt excited! "Tomorrow morning we'll be home!" I told the cats. I wondered why the cats were not as excited as I was.

I was sort of scared, too—scared of the big city and elevators and freeways and of seeing millions of people again.

The sky in the east was beginning to lighten. Soon it would be dawn. I went into the cabin and shaved—my first shave since leaving the Galápagos. When I had set out on my voyage, I had never shaved. Now I could grow quite a beard.

Kili, Pooh and Piglet were still sleeping on my bunk. I woke them up.

"Come on, you lazy cats," I said. "It's time for breakfast. I can't have you looking like alley waifs when you meet my family and friends tomorrow."

(Above right) *Patti and her father.* (Below) *I spend last night wrapped in a blanket.*

The cats did not like being awakened, so I opened my last can of boned chicken. They sure appreciated this breakfast.

Kili, Pooh and Piglet came up on deck with me. All four of us looked at the lovely sunrise.

Then I turned *Dove* between the breakwaters into Long Beach-San Pedro harbor—the same harbor entrance I had left so long ago. I saw a powered cruiser coming fast towards me. Standing on the foredeck was Patti. Her hair was streaming behind her in the wind.

"Hi, Robin!"

"Hi, Patti!"

Those were our first words. Patti was not allowed to climb aboard *Dove* until I had cleared customs. But she leaned over the railing of the cruiser and passed across a breakfast tray. There was half a melon with a cherry on it, cottage cheese and a delicious sweet roll.

A helicopter hovered overhead. Press and television people were taking pictures of my homecoming. Suddenly the outer harbor was filled with yachts. They were like a swarm of butterflies coming towards me. This was the day of the famous Ensenada yacht race.

The yachtsmen seemed to know who I was. They waved and cheered as they sailed past *Dove*. "Welcome home, Robin," they shouted.

It was just after eight o'clock in the morning when I threw a line to someone on the Long Beach marina and *Dove* nudged into the berth and came to rest. My journey had taken 1,739 days. I had traveled 30,600 miles.

It was quite a reception. Beyond the heads of the newsmen I could see Patti, my mother and father. The reporters shouted questions at me and the TV cameras zoomed in. Kili, Pooh and Piglet came up on deck to find out what all the fuss was about.

"What does it feel like to be the youngest sailor to have circled the world?" asked one reporter.

"I haven't thought about that," I replied.

"Would you do it again?" asked another reporter.

"No," I replied, "because there are so many other things I want to do."

Patti had come out to the harbor wall to welcome me home; she handed over a lovely breakfast. Then I lowered Dove's *sails.*

The reporter's questions came at me one after the other, but all I wanted to do was to hug Patti, Mom and Dad. (Below) That's Mom.

"What have you proved?" asked a reporter fiercely.

"That the world is really round," I grinned. Of course there was more to it than that.

I had not talked to anyone for 38 days, and my tongue would just not catch up with my thoughts. I guess the reporters thought I was as dumb as Kili, Pooh and Piglet. The three cats were frightened by the crowd standing around *Dove*. When the press photographers started shooting pictures, the cats dashed back into the cabin. I wanted to do the same thing.

At last the reporters' questions came to an end. The customs people found no contraband, so they allowed me to leave the boat. It was just great to hug Patti again and Mom and Dad.

139

If this had been a fairy story, I guess Patti and I would have sailed off into the sunset. It was good to be home!

One thing I didn't tell the reporters, and which I can say now, is that if it had not been for Patti and for God's care for me, I would not have completed my voyage around the world.

Soon Patti and I were alone together—except for the cats. Patti drove Kili, Pooh, Piglet and me to my parents' home in Newport Beach. I wasn't allowed to drive because I had never driven a car. We thought this was funny. I had traveled around the world but I did not know how to drive around the block! There were so many things I still had to learn—but the most scary thing of all was learning to drive along the Los Angeles freeways.

Not long after I reached home our baby was born on Catalina Island, 20 miles off the coast from Los Angeles. We called her Quimby. It was a name we had first thought of in the Galápagos.

I began to ask myself what our next adventure should be. Patti said, "In one way our life together is just beginning for us, isn't it? I'm sure our next adventure is going to be just as exciting as sailing around the world."

Patti was right. What happened to us after this was so unexpected and so full of joy and excitement.

But that is another story. Perhaps sometime I will write a book about our next adventure—a book just like this one.

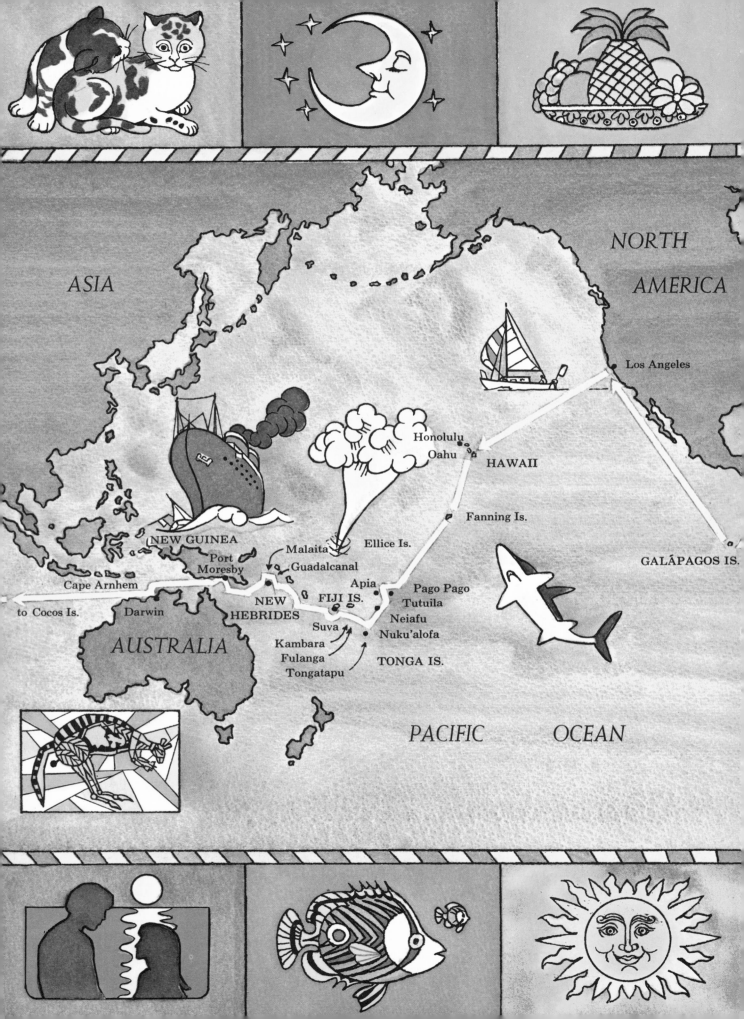